All-Year-Round
KNITTING
for Little Sweethearts

68 PATTERNS
for Everyday, Parties, and Special Times

Hanne Andreassen Hjelmås

Torunn Steinsland

Creators of KlompeLompe

Photography by Hanne Andreassen Hjelmås

SCHIFFER
PUBLISHING
4880 Lower Valley Road · Atglen, PA 19310

Other Schiffer Books by the Authors:

Knitting for Little Sweethearts,
ISBN 978-0-7643-5627-8

**Other Schiffer Books on
Related Subjects:**

*Create Naturally: Go Outside and
Rediscover Nature with 15 Makers*, Marcia
Young, ISBN 978-0-7643-6434-1

Weave It! 15 Fun Weaving Projects for Kids,
Maria Sigma, ISBN 978-0-7643-6065-7

*Paint-Your-Own Watercolor Garland:
Illustrations by Kristy Rice*, Kristy Rice,
ISBN 978-0-7643-6315-3

English edition copyright © 2022 by Schiffer
Publishing, Ltd.

Originally published as *KlompeLompe:
Strikk Året Rundt* © J.M. Stenersens Forlag
2017

Copyright © Hanne Andreassen Hjelmås,
Torunn Steinsland, 2017

Library of Congress Control Number:
2022932596

Translated from the Norwegian by
Carol Huebescher Rhoades
Designed by Anne Vines
Photography: Hanne Andreassen Hjelmås
Type set in Nimbus Sans

ISBN: 978-0-7643-6507-2
Printed in India

Published by Schiffer Publishing, Ltd.
4880 Lower Valley Road
Atglen, PA 19310
Phone: (610) 593-1777; Fax: (610) 593-2002
Email: Info@schifferbooks.com
Web: www.schifferbooks.com

For our complete selection of fine books on
this and related subjects, please visit our
website at www.schifferbooks.com. You may
also write for a free catalog.

Schiffer Publishing's titles are available at
special discounts for bulk purchases for
sales promotions or premiums. Special
editions, including personalized covers,
corporate imprints, and excerpts, can
be created in large quantities for special
needs. For more information, contact the
publisher.

We are always looking for people to write
books on new and related subjects. If you
have an idea for a book, please contact us
at proposals@schifferbooks.com.

Contents

≪⎯ Party Dress Cardigan, color A: 6521, color B:
   1013

Introduction

We wear knitted garments for all sorts of reasons and in all seasons. Our intent for this book was to design for a whole year of wearable garments, from everyday to parties and from summer to winter. Knitted garments can vary endlessly, and you'll find a wide variety in this book.

Since one of us was pregnant and had the child while the book was in process, it was natural to include a christening dress, an idea we've had for a long time. A christening dress in KlompeLompe style, simple but pretty. That also inspired our ideas about festive clothes. There are many fine patterns available for knitted *bunads* (Norwegian folk costumes, worn for special occasions here) and party outfits, but we wanted to make a series in our style and with our colors, and we are so satisfied! These garments have many pattern motifs and are knitted on fine needles, so that they'll be delicate and fine. Most of all, we have plenty of typical KlompeLompe clothes in the book, such as quick cap projects, simple everyday garments, and sweet baby clothes.

It's obvious that knitting style coincides with one's life situation.

We were inspired by our children and noticed that the oldest had become older. Several of the children's garments therefore go up into larger sizes, all the way up to 14 years. Baby garment production has also increased here at KlompeLompe since little Olivia was born.

KlompeLompe cardigans in adult sizes have been favorite garments we wear a lot. For that reason, we wanted to broaden the adult collection with several cardigans and other adult pieces. Knitting for adults takes more time than for children, but you'll get a personal garment with your own color choice, which you can wear for many years.

We list the yarns that were used for the knits in the photographs, but because yarn companies change their lines, it's inevitable that some of the yarns may be discontinued. If you can't find the yarn noted, or if you have different preferences, simply use a similar weight and type of yarn.

Our followers who knit our patterns are an important source of inspiration for us, and we've paid attention to their suggestions about garments and sizes.

We hope you will find knitting fun and comfort with this book. Perhaps try a new challenge or find a new easy favorite!

Knitting Tips from Grandmother

Hanne's grandmother taught her how to knit when Hanne was a little girl, and her grandmother's tips have remained with her along the way and are well remembered. Grandmother said that laying the garments under a damp hand towel to block them was gentler than pressing them with a steam iron. Garments knitted with texture patterns especially benefit from this method of finishing because the pattern is not pressed down. For example, seed stitch will show well. There is something magic about lifting up the towel after a garment has lain under it for a few hours, because then you can see that what had perhaps been uneven and crumpled knitting has now become even, smooth, and pretty. Some garments do need to be steam pressed, and, if so, it will be stated in the pattern instructions. However, we usually abide by Grandmother's tips for most of the garments we make.

Grandmother also said that you should not be afraid to rip out. You will have spent so much time on a garment that, if you don't rip out an error, it will irritate you later on. What differentiates a beginner from an experienced knitter is not necessarily that the experienced one never make mistakes, but that she knows when to rip out and reknit. She knows it is totally worth the trouble.

KNITTING GAUGE
Some people knit tightly while others knit loosely. You should always check the gauge given in a pattern. Make a gauge swatch so that you can be certain that your knitted measurements will match those given in the pattern. Here's what to do:

Cast on a few stitches more than given for the gauge over 4 inches (10 centimeters). Work the swatch in stockinette or the technique used in the pattern. Count how many stitches are in 4 inches (10 cm) horizontally and check to see if your knitting matches the recommended gauge. If you have too many stitches, go up a needle size, and, if there are too few stitches, try smaller-size needles. For a multicolor pattern, it is especially important to check the gauge since many knitters work too tightly in two-color stranded knitting. One way to correct this is to go up by a US needle size or by 0.5 mm whenever you are working two-color stranded knitting.

You might think that a couple of stitches' difference in gauge won't affect your work, but even a two-stitch difference per 4 inches (10 cm) can make the garment an entire size larger or smaller.

If you have a tendency to cast on tightly, try casting on over two needles held together. Carefully remove the extra needle before you begin knitting.

CHOOSING THE YARN
We have recommended yarn for all of our patterns and have also recommended alternatives for many of the designs. If you want to use another yarn, that's fine as long as the gauge matches. Keep in mind that caps made with cotton yarn have less elasticity and do not hold their shape as well as Merino wool, for example. In larger garments, alpaca will feel heavier and perhaps stretch more than sheep's wool. It's fun to see how different a garment can be by choosing various yarn qualities.

Don't forget to follow the washing instructions for the yarn so that the garment will look nice for as long as possible.

TOOLS
You don't need very many tools for knitting, but there are a few helpful items you might want. Small plastic stitch markers are very handy. It's easy to move them from needle to needle, and they stay in place on the surface of the needle. You could use small loops of yarn instead.

It's worthwhile to invest in good-quality knitting needles. We normally use bamboo or wood needles because they are easier on our wrists and are quieter. That way, we avoid complaints from our partners when we knit as we watch TV.

We recommend a knitting mill for I-cords since it speeds up the work considerably.

NEW TECHNIQUES
If your work develops ladders when you are knitting in the round with double-pointed needles, we recommend that you try out the magic loop method. For that method, you knit with an extralong circular needle, preferably 32 inches (80 cm) long. Learn more about magic loop on our video at klompelompe.no.

KNITTING HELP
If you have trouble with a pattern, go to the yarn store for some help. Most of the people who work at yarn stores are experienced knitters and have many good tips to share. Don't be afraid to get help on the internet if there is something you think is difficult. There are innumerable videos available with good explanations of various knitting techniques. All good resources, in case you don't have a knitting grandmother in the neighborhood.

ABBREVIATIONS

KNITTING

as est	as established; that is, continue in pattern
BO	bind off (= British cast off)
Cc	contrast color (pattern color)
cm	centimeter(s)
CO	cast on
dpn	double-pointed needle
g	grams
in	inches
k	knit
kf&b	knit into front and then back of same stitch = 1 stitch increased
k2tog	knit 2 together = right-leaning decrease; 1 stitch decreased
k3tog	knit 3 together = right-leaning decrease; 2 stitches decreased
k4tog	knit 4 together = right-leaning decrease; 3 stitches decreased
LLI	Left-lifted Increase = knit into left side of stitch below stitch just worked
m	meter(s)
M1	Make 1 = lift strand between 2 stitches onto left needle and knit into back loop = 1 stitch increased; stitch is twisted
M1p	Make 1 purl = lift strand between 2 stitches onto left needle and purl into back loop = 1 st increase; stitch I twisted
MC	main color (background color)
mm	millimeters
p	purl
pm	place marker
psso	pass slipped stitch over
rem	remain/remaining
rep	repeat(s)
rnd(s)	round(s)
RLI	right-lifted Increase = knit into right side of stitch below loop on needle = 1 stitch increased
RS	right side
sl	slip
sl m	slip marker
ssk	(sl 1 knitwise) 2 times, insert left needle into sts and knit together through back loops = left-leaning decrease; 1 stitch decreased
st(s)	stitch(es)
tbl	through back loop
WS	wrong side
wyb	with yarn held in back
wyf	with yarn held in front
yd(s)	yard(s)
yo	yarnover
* - *	repeat the sequence between asterisks

CROCHET

ch	chain
dc	double crochet (= British treble crochet)
hdc	half double crochet (= British half treble crochet)
sc	single crochet (= British double crochet)
sl st	slip stitch
tr	treble (= British double treble)

FELTING

Some projects in this book are felted. It is exciting to see how a garment changes size and structure after felting. We have tried two different felting techniques.

Felting in the washing machine: Set the machine to the regular colored-wash cycle at 122°F (50°C). Toss a small terry cloth towel or something similar into the machine along with the garment to be felted. Use wool-safe soap. Set spin cycle on high. If the garment is still too large after felting, try another cycle in the machine.

Felting in the dryer: Wash garment at 122°F (50°C) without spin cycle.

Squeeze out water and put garment into dryer. Check the size of the garment occasionally as it dries.

Winter

Winter Pine Cone Onesie

This delicately patterned overall is bound to be one of those things worn every single day all through winter. It's that great!

SIZES: 1–3 months (6–9 months, 1, 2 years)

FINISHED MEASUREMENTS
Chest: Approx. 18¼ (19, 21¼, 22) in [46 (48, 54, 56) cm]
Total Length: Approx. 18¼ (21, 25¼, 28¼) in [46 (53, 64, 72) cm]

MATERIALS
YARN: Sandnes Garn KlompeLompe Tynn Merinoull (fine Merino wool) [CYCA #1 – fingering, 100% Merino wool, 191 yd (175 m) / 50 g]

YARN COLORS AND AMOUNTS:
Color A 6521 (MC): 50 (50, 50, 100) g
Color B 2652: 150 (150, 200, 200)
Color C 1013: 50 (50, 50, 50) g
NEEDLES: US sizes 1.5 and 2.5 (2.5 and 3 mm): 16 and 24 in (40 and 60 cm) circulars and sets of 5 dpn
NOTIONS: 6 (7, 7, 8) buttons

GAUGE: 27 sts on larger-size needles = 4 in (10 cm).
Adjust needle size to obtain correct gauge if necessary.

The onesie is worked from the top down.

BODY

With smaller-size circular and color A, CO 85 (89, 89, 93) sts, Work back and forth in k1, p1 ribbing for 1¼ in (3 cm).

Change to larger-size circular. Knit 1 row and CO 6 sts at end of row for steek. Steek sts are not included on the pattern chart or in any stitch counts. Now join to begin working in the round.

Knit 1 rnd, *at the same time*, increasing 36 (40, 48, 52) sts evenly spaced around = 121 (129, 137, 145) sts. Knit 1 rnd.

Begin following chart A for chosen size. After completing charted rows, you should have 211 (225, 239, 253) sts + the 6 steek sts. With MC, knit 0 (1, 2, 4) rnds. Knit 1 more rnd, adjusting stitch count evenly spaced around to 211 (221, 243, 257) sts.

Set aside sleeve sts as follows: K27 (28, 32, 34), place next 52, 54, 56, 60 sts on a holder, CO 7 sts for underarm, k53 (57, 67, 69), place next 52, 54, 56, 60 sts on a holder, CO 7 sts for underarm, k27 (28, 32, 34) + steek sts.

FRONT AND BACK

You should now have 121 (127, 145, 151) sts on the needle. With color A, knit 8 (8, 10, 10) rnds. Now work following chart B.

Continue until onesie measures 11½ (13, 14½, 16¼) in [29 (33, 37, 41) cm]. Knit 1 rnd and, *at the same time*, BO the 6 steek sts.

On the next rnd, pm as follows: K58 (61, 70, 73), pm, k5, pm, k58 (61, 70, 73), pm, CO 5 sts, pm = marker on each side of the 5 center front and back sts.

Now increase 1 st on each side of the 5 center sts at front and back = 4 sts increased. Rep the increases on every 4th rnd a total of 4 (4, 5, 6) times.

(Stop working lice on the 5 marked sts on front and back, but work new increased lice sts outside markers into lice pattern.)

Knit 1 rnd and BO the 5 sts at center front and back = 66 (69, 80, 85) sts rem for each leg.

LEGS (CONTINUED IN LICE PATTERN)

Pm at split. Decrease as follows: Knit until 3 sts before marker, sl 1, k1, psso, knit until 1 st after marker, k2tog.

Rep the decrease rnd every ¾ in (2 cm) a total of 5 (5, 6, 8) times and then knit until leg measures 4¾ (6, 7½, 9½) in [12 (15, 19, 24) cm] = 56 (59, 68, 69) sts rem. Knit 1 rnd, *at the same time*, decreasing 16 (17, 20, 21) sts evenly spaced around = 40 (42, 48, 48) sts rem.

Change to smaller-size dpn and work in

k1, p1 ribbing for 1¼ in (3 cm). BO in ribbing. Make the other leg the same way.

SLEEVES (WORKED WITH COLOR A)

With color A and larger-size dpn, CO 4 sts, knit the 52, 54, 56, 60 sts from holder, CO 3 sts. Join and work around. Always purl the 1st st (marked st) as center of underarm. With color A, knit 8 (8, 10, 10) rnds.

Now work following chart C.
When sleeve measures 1¼ (1¼, 1⅜, 1⅜) in. [3 (3, 3.5, 3.5) cm], shape as follows:

Knit until 2 sts before marked st, sl 1, k1, psso, p1 (marked st), k2tog.

Rep decrease rnd approx. every ¾ in (2 cm) until 49 (49, 49, 49) sts rem. Continue without further shaping until sleeve measures 5¼ (6¼, 7½, 8¾) in [13 (16, 19, 22) cm].

Knit 2 rnds; BO marked st. Knit 1 rnd, *at the same time*, decreasing 8 (6, 4, 4) sts evenly spaced around.

Change to smaller-size dpn and work around in k1, p1 ribbing for 1¼ in (3 cm). BO in ribbing.

Make the 2nd sleeve the same way.

FINISHING

Machine-stitch 2 fine lines on each side of center steek. Carefully cut steek open up center st.

With color (MC) and smaller-size circular, pick up and knit sts along 1 front edge—picking up about 3 sts for every 4 rows. Work back and forth in k1, p1 ribbing for 8 rows. BO in ribbing—make sure bind-off is not too tight. On the boy's version, make the buttonholes on the left front band and on the right band for a girl. Make 6 (7, 7, 8) buttonholes evenly spaced on band.

Buttonhole: BO 2 sts on row 3; on row 4, CO 2 sts over each gap.

Fold cut edges down on WS and sew down with small stitches. If it is difficult to make a fine edge, you can knit a facing over the steek. Pick up and knit sts as you did for front bands. Work back and forth in stockinette until band is wide enough to cover cut edges. BO and sew facing over steek edges. So it won't show, sew down facings with MC.

Seam underarms. Sew down short lower ends of button bands. Sew on buttons. Weave in all ends neatly on WS.

Lay a damp towel over onesie and leave until completely dry.

Chart A
(1–3 and 6–9 months)

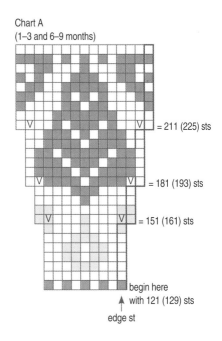

= 211 (225) sts

= 181 (193) sts

= 151 (161) sts

begin here with 121 (129) sts
edge st

Chart A
(1 and 2 years)

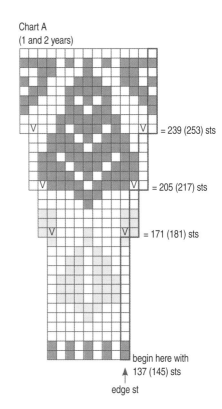

= 239 (253) sts

= 205 (217) sts

= 171 (181) sts

begin here with 137 (145) sts
edge st

Chart B

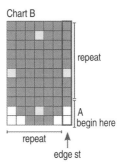

repeat

A
begin here

repeat

edge st

Chart C

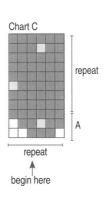

repeat

A

repeat

begin here

☐ Color A

■ Color B

☐ Color C

Ⅴ Increase here. Increase with M1: lift strand between 2 sts and knit into back loop with color A.

Alternate color suggestions:
Color A: 6521; color B: 6571; color C: 1013 ⟶ ≫

Winter Pine Cone Pullover for Women

SIZES: XS (S, M, L, XL)

FINISHED MEASUREMENTS
Chest: Approx. 34 (36, 37¾, 43¼, 45½) in [86 (91, 96, 110, 115.5) cm]
Total Length: Approx. 26 (26½, 26¾, 27½, 28) in [66 (67, 68, 70, 71) cm]

MATERIALS
YARN: Sandnes Garn KlompeLompe Tynn Merinoull (fine Merino wool) [CYCA #1 – fingering, 100% Merino wool, 191 yd (175 m) / 50 g]
YARN COLORS AND AMOUNTS:
Color A 6521 (MC): 350 (350, 400, 450, 450) g
Color B 6571: 50 (50, 50, 50, 50) g
Color C 1013: 50 (50, 50, 50, 50) g
NEEDLES: US sizes 1.5 and 2.5 (2.5 and 3 mm): 16 and 24 in (40 and 60 cm) circulars and sets of 5 dpn

GAUGE: 27 sts on larger-size needles = 4 in (10 cm).
Adjust needle size to obtain correct gauge if necessary.

The pullover is worked from the top down, in the round on circular needles.

With smaller-size circular and color A, CO 130 (144, 154, 162, 166) sts, Join, being careful not to twist cast-on row; pm for beginning of rnd. Work around in k1, p1 ribbing for 1½ in (4 cm).

Change to larger-size circular and knit 1 rnd.

Knit 1 rnd, increasing 22 (16, 14, 22, 26) sts evenly spaced around = 152 (160,168, 184, 192) sts. Begin pattern following chart A.

After completing charted rows, you should have 304 (320, 336, 368, 384) sts. Knit 10 rnds with MC and then knit 1 rnd increasing 20 (24, 22, 30, 34) sts evenly spaced around = 324 (344, 358, 398, 418) sts. Knit 8 (8, 10, 12, 14) rnds.

Knit 1 rnd, increasing 22 (30, 38, 44, 44) sts evenly spaced around = 346 (374, 396, 442, 462) sts.

Set aside sleeve sts as follows:

Place the next 69 (76, 80, 85, 87) sts on a holder for sleeve, CO 12 sts for underarm, k104 (111, 118, 136, 144) (front), place the next 69 (76, 80, 85, 87) sts on a holder for sleeve, CO 12 sts for underarm, k104 (111, 118, 136, 144) (back).

FRONT AND BACK

232 (246, 260, 296, 312) sts rem.

With MC, knit around until piece measures 22 (22½, 22¾, 23¾, 24) in [56 (57, 58, 60, 61) cm].

Work following chart B and then knit 1 rnd with color A (MC).

Change to smaller-size circular and work k1, p1 ribbing for 3¼ in (8 cm). BO in ribbing on last rnd.

SLEEVES

With larger-size dpn and MC, CO 6 sts, knit the held 69 (76, 80, 85, 87) sleeve sts, CO 6 sts.

The sleeve is knitted around on dpn. Always purl the 1st (marked) st for center of underarm.

Work around as est until sleeve measures ¾ in (2 cm). Now begin shaping sleeve as follows:

Knit until 2 sts before marked purl st, sl 1, k1, psso, p1, k2tog.

Decrease the same way every 1¼ (1, 1, ¾, 1) in [3 (2.5, 2.5, 2, 2.5) cm] until 55 (56, 60, 59, 61) sts rem.

Continue without further shaping until sleeve is 15¾ in (40 cm) long or desired length. Knit 1 rnd, decreasing 1 (0, 0, 1, 1) st.

Work pattern following chart B and then knit 1 rnd with color A.

Change to smaller-size dpn and work k1, p1 ribbing for 3¼ in (8 cm). BO in ribbing.

Make 2nd sleeve the same way.

FINISHING

Seam underarms. Weave in all ends neatly on WS.

Lay a damp towel over pullover and leave until completely dry.

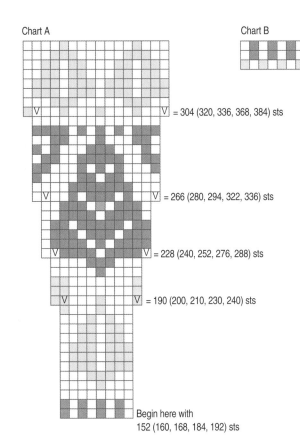

Chart A

Chart B

Begin here

V = 304 (320, 336, 368, 384) sts

V = 266 (280, 294, 322, 336) sts

V = 228 (240, 252, 276, 288) sts

V = 190 (200, 210, 230, 240) sts

Begin here with
152 (160, 168, 184, 192) sts

☐ Color A

■ Color B

☐ Color C

V Increase here. Increase with M1: lift strand between 2 sts and knit into back loop with color A.

Alternate color suggestion: Color A: 6571; color B: 1013; color C: 6521

Winter Pine Cone Pullover for Children

After countless walks in the woods with pockets full of pine cones and small stones in the snow-deprived winter landscape on Karmøy, the idea for this pattern and its name, winter pine cone, came to me. According to the children, pine cones can be used for everything; a toy animal as well as building blocks.

SIZES: 1 (2, 4, 6, 8, 10, 12) years

FINISHED MEASUREMENTS
Chest: Approx. 21¾ (22, 24½ , 27½, 29½, 30¼, 32) in [55 (56, 62, 70, 75, 77, 81.5) cm]
Total Length: Approx. 13 (15, 16½, 18¼, 19½, 20½, 22) in [33 (38, 42, 46.5, 49.5, 52, 56) cm]

MATERIALS
YARN: Sandnes Garn KlompeLompe Tynn Merinoull (fine Merino wool) [CYCA #1 – fingering, 100% Merino wool, 191 yd (175 m) / 50 g]
YARN COLORS AND AMOUNTS:
Color A 7251 (MC): 150 (150, 150, 200, 200, 250, 300) g
Color B 1013: 50 (50, 50, 50, 50) g
Color C 6521: 50 (50, 50, 50, 50) g
NEEDLES: US sizes 1.5 and 2.5 (2.5 and 3 mm): 16 and 24 in (40 and 60 cm) circulars and sets of 5 dpn

GAUGE: 27 sts on larger-size needles = 4 in (10 cm).
Adjust needle size to obtain correct gauge if necessary.

The pullover is worked from the top down, in the round on circular needles.

With smaller-size circular and color A, CO 90 (94, 100, 100, 108, 108, 114) sts, Join, being careful not to twist cast-on row; pm for beginning of rnd. Work around in k1, p1 ribbing for 1¼ (1¼, 1¼, 1⅜, 1⅜, 1⅜, 1⅜) in [3 (3, 3, 3.5, 3.5, 3.5, 3.5) cm].

Change to larger-size circular and knit 1 rnd.
Knit 1 rnd, increasing 46 (50, 44, 52, 52, 52, 54) sts evenly spaced around = 136 (144,144, 152, 160, 160, 168) sts.
Begin pattern following chart A.
After completing charted rows, you should have 238 (252, 252, 304, 320, 320, 336) sts.
With MC, knit 0 (4, 3, 5, 8, 8, 8) rnds and then knit 1 rnd increasing 8 (6, 26, 0, 0, 12, 8) sts evenly spaced around = 246 (258, 278, 304, 320, 332, 344) sts.
Size 4 years: Knit 4 rnds.
Sizes 10 (12) years: Knit 4 (6) rnds.

Set aside sleeve sts as follows:
Place the next 56 (60, 62, 64, 66, 69, 69) sts on a holder for sleeve, CO 7 sts for underarm, k67 (69, 77, 88, 94, 97, 103) (front), place the next 56 (60, 62, 64, 66, 69, 69) sts on a holder for sleeve, CO 7 sts for underarm, k67 (69, 77, 88, 94, 97, 103) (back).

FRONT AND BACK

148 (152, 168, 190, 202, 208, 220) sts rem. With MC, knit around until piece measures 11 (13, 14½, 16¼, 17¼, 18¼, 19¾) in [28 (33, 37, 41, 44, 46, 50) cm]. Knit 1 rnd, decreasing 1 st at each side = 2 sts decreased. Work following chart B and then knit 1 rnd with color A.
Change to smaller-size circular and work k1, p1 ribbing for 1¼ (1¼, 1¼, 1⅜, 1⅜, 1½, 1½) in [3 (3, 3, 3.5, 3.5, 4, 4) cm]. BO in ribbing on last rnd.

SLEEVES

With larger-size dpn and MC, CO 4 sts, knit the held 56 (60, 62, 64, 66, 69, 69) sleeve sts, CO 3 sts.
The sleeve is knitted around on dpn. Always purl the 1st (marked) st for center of underarm.
Work around as est until sleeve measures ¾ in (2 cm). Now begin shaping sleeve as follows:
Knit until 2 sts before marked purl st, sl 1, k1, psso, p1, k2tog.
Decrease the same way every ⅝ (¾, ¾, 1, 1, 1¼, 1⅜) in [1.5 (2, 2, 2.5, 2.5, 3, 3.5) cm] until 45 (49, 49, 51, 51, 56, 56) sts rem.
Continue without further shaping until sleeve is 6¾ (8, 9, 10¼, 11½, 12¾, 14¼) in [17 (20, 23, 26, 29, 32, 36) cm] long or desired length. Knit 1 rnd, decreasing 1 (1, 1, 1, 1, 0, 0) st.

Work pattern following chart B and then knit 1 rnd with color A.

Change to smaller-size dpn and work k1, p1 ribbing for 1¼ (1¼, 1¼, 1⅜, 1⅜, 1½, 1½) in [3 (3, 3, 3.5, 4, 4) cm]. BO in ribbing.

Make 2nd sleeve the same way.

FINISHING

Seam underarms. Weave in all ends neatly on WS.

Lay a damp towel over pullover and leave until completely dry.

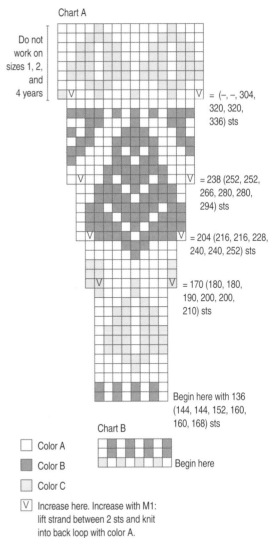

Chart A

Do not work on sizes 1, 2, and 4 years

= (−, −, 304, 320, 320, 336) sts

= 238 (252, 252, 266, 280, 280, 294) sts

= 204 (216, 216, 228, 240, 240, 252) sts

= 170 (180, 180, 190, 200, 200, 210) sts

Begin here with 136 (144, 144, 152, 160, 160, 168) sts

Chart B

Begin here

☐ Color A

▨ Color B

☐ Color C

Ⓥ Increase here. Increase with M1: lift strand between 2 sts and knit into back loop with color A.

Winter Pine Cone Pants

A pair of pants to go
with both the Winter
Pine Cone Pullover and
Winter Pine Cone Jacket.

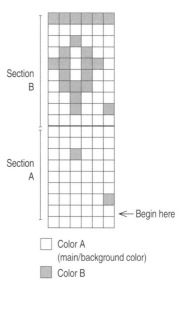

Section
B

Section
A

← Begin here

☐ Color A
   (main/background color)
▨ Color B

«   Winter Pine Cone Pullover, color A: 1042,
   color B: 6571, color C: 1013

SIZES: 0–2 months (3, 6–9, 12, 18 months, 2, 4, 6 years)

FINISHED MEASUREMENTS

Waist: Approx. 17½ (19½, 19½, 20½, 20½, 21¾, 21⅞, 22½) in [44.5 (49.5, 49.5, 52, 52, 55, 55.5, 57) cm]

Total Length: Approx. 12¾ (14¼, 15¾, 17, 19, 19¾, 23, 26½) in [32 (36.5, 40, 43.5, 48, 50.5, 58.5, 67.5) cm]

MATERIALS

YARN: Sandnes Garn KlompeLompe Tynn Merinoull (fine Merino wool) [CYCA #1 – fingering, 100% Merino wool, 191 yd (175 m) / 50 g]

YARN COLORS AND AMOUNTS:

Color A 6571 (MC): 100 (100, 100, 100, 150, 150, 150, 150) g

Color B 1013: 50 (50, 50, 50, 50, 50, 50, 50) g

NEEDLES: US sizes 1.5 and 2.5 (2.5 and 3 mm): 16 in (40 cm) circulars and sets of 5 dpn or use 32 in (80 cm) circular for magic loop (see video on magic loop technique on klompelompe.no).

GAUGE: 27 sts on larger-size needles = 4 in (10 cm).

Adjust needle size to obtain correct gauge if necessary.

The pants are worked top down and knitted in the round.

With smaller-size needle and color A (MC):, CO 120 (134, 134, 140, 140, 148, 150, 154) sts. Join, being careful not to twist cast-on row; pm for beginning of rnd. Work around in k1, p1 ribbing for 1 (1, 1, 1, 1¼, 1¼, 1¼, 1¼) in [2.5 (2.5, 2.5, 2.5, 3, 3, 3, 3) cm].

On the next rnd, make eyelets as follows:

Sizes 0–2 months:

5 sts ribbing, k2tog, yo, *10 sts ribbing, k2tog, yo*; work * to * 9 times, 5 sts ribbing.

Sizes 3 and 6–9 months:

6 sts ribbing, k2tog, yo, *11 sts ribbing, k2tog, yo*; work * to * 4 times, 14 sts ribbing, k2tog, yo, rep * to * 4 times, 6 sts ribbing.

Sizes 12 and 18 months:

6 sts ribbing, k2tog, yo, *12 sts ribbing, k2tog, yo*; work * to * 9 times, 6 sts ribbing.

Size 2 years:

5 sts ribbing, k2tog, yo, *10 sts ribbing, k2tog, yo*; work * to * 5 times, 14 sts ribbing, k2tog, yo, rep * to * 5 times, 5 sts ribbing

Size 4 years:

5 sts ribbing, k2tog, yo, *10 sts ribbing, k2tog, yo*; work * to * 5 times, 16 sts ribbing, k2tog, yo, rep * to * 5 times, 5 sts ribbing.

Size 6 years:

5 sts ribbing, k2tog, yo, *9 sts ribbing, k2tog, yo*; work * to * 13 times, 4 sts ribbing.

Work in ribbing for 1 (1, 1, 1, 1¼, 1¼, 1¼, 1¼) in [2.5 (2.5, 2.5, 2.5, 3, 3, 3, 3) cm]. Change to larger size circular, Knit 1 rnd, increasing 6 (4, 10, 4, 10, 8, 6, 8) sts evenly spaced around = 126 (138, 144, 144, 150, 156, 156, 162) sts.

Now work short rows to raise the back. (When turning, wrap yarn around next st before you turn, and, when you come to the st later, knit st together with its wrap) K10; turn, p20; turn, k25; turn, p30; turn, k35; turn, p40; turn, k45; turn, p50; turn, k25 = beginning of rnd.

The 1st st is center back. Knit 1 rnd and then work following chart.

When piece measures 5¼ (6, 6¼, 6¾, 7, 7½, 8¼, 9¾) in [13 (15, 16, 17, 18, 19, 21, 25) cm], pm on each side of the center front 7 sts and back = 4 markers. Increase 1 st with M1 before and after each group of 7 marked sts at front and back = 4 sts increased on rnd.

Increase the same way every 3rd rnd a total of 6 times = 150 (162,168, 168, 174, 180, 186) sts.

Note: Continue the lice pattern between front and back markers and work new sts into lice pattern.

On the next rnd, BO the 7 marked sts at front and back. Work each leg separately = 68 (74, 77, 77, 80, 83, 83, 86) sts. On the 1st rnd, decrease 1 st centered under leg for sizes 6-9 and 12 months, 2 and 4 years = 68 (74, 76, 76, 80, 82, 82, 86) sts rem.

Pm at beginning of rnd. Continue with lice pattern.

Work for ⅜ in (1 cm) and then decrease as follows: K1, k2tog, knit until 3 sts before marker, sl 1, k1, psso, k1.

Rep the decrease rnd every ¾ (¾, ¾, ¾, 1¼, 1¼, 1¼, 1¼) in [2 (2, 2, 2, 3, 3, 3, 3) cm] a total of 4 (4, 5, 5, 4, 5, 5, 7) times = 60 (66, 66, 66, 72, 72, 72, 72) sts rem. The lice pattern gradually disappears.

Continue in lice pattern until leg measures approx. 3¼ (4¼, 5¼, 6¼, 7¼, 8, 10¼, 12¼) in [8.5 (11, 13.5, 16, 18.5, 20, 26, 31) cm] and you have completed either row 4 or 8 in pattern on chart A. Now work chart B. Make sure that the pattern in chart B matches the lice from chart A.

With MC, knit 1 rnd.

Knit 1 rnd, decreasing 20 sts evenly spaced around = 40 (46, 46, 46, 52, 52, 52, 52) sts rem.

Change to smaller-size dpn and work around in k1, p2 ribbing for 1½ (1½ 1½, 1½, 2, 2, 2, 2) in [4 (4, 4, 4, 5, 5, 5, 5) cm]. BO in ribbing.

Make the 2nd leg the same way.

FINISHING

Seam crotch with mattress stitch (see page 124).

Weave in all ends neatly on WS. With color B, make an I-cord tie for waist.

Little Winter Pine Cone Cardigan

With the Winter Pine Cone Pullover as our starting point, we made a simpler cardigan for baby. In the same series you'll find pants, a cap, mittens, and socks.

Level 3

SIZES: 0–1 (3, 6–12, 18–24) months

FINISHED MEASUREMENTS
Chest: Approx. 20 (21, 25¼, 27¼) in [51 (53.5, 64.5, 69) cm]
Total Length: Approx. 10 (10¾, 12½, 14¾) in [25.5 (27.5, 31.5, 37.5) cm]

MATERIALS
YARN: Sandnes Garn KlompeLompe Tynn Merinoull (fine Merino wool) [CYCA #1 – fingering, 100% Merino wool, 191 yd (175 m) / 50 g]
YARN COLORS AND AMOUNTS:
Color A 4331 (MC): 50 (100, 150, 200) g
Color B 1013: 50 (50, 50, 50) g
NEEDLES: US sizes 1.5 and 2.5 (2.5 and 3 mm): 16 or 24 in (40 or 60 cm) circulars and sets of 5 dpn or use 32 in (80 cm) circular for magic loop (see video on magic loop technique on klompelompe.no).
NOTIONS: 6 (6, 7, 7) buttons

GAUGE: 27 sts on larger-size needles = 4 in (10 cm).
Adjust needle size to obtain correct gauge if necessary.

The sweater is worked top down, beginning back and forth on a circular.

With color A (MC) and smaller-size circular, CO 75 (81, 81, 85) sts. Work back and forth in k1, p1 ribbing for 1 (1¼, 1¼, 1¼) in [2.5 (3, 3, 3) cm]. Change to larger-size circular. Knit 1 row, increasing 40 (40, 40, 48) sts evenly spaced across = 115 (121, 121, 133) sts. At end of row, CO 7 sts for steek. Steek sts are not included in any st counts or on the chart.

Now join to work in the round.
Knit 1 rnd and then work following chart A.

After completing charted rows, continue with color A = 191(201, 201, 221) sts.

Knit 1 rnd.
Knit 1 rnd, increasing 20 (20, 30, 30) sts evenly spaced across = 211 (221, 231, 251) sts.
Knit 1 (4, 6, 6) rnds. Knit 0 (0, 1, 1) rnd, increasing 0 (0, 30, 30) sts evenly spaced around = 211 (221, 261, 281) sts.
Knit 0 (0, 4, 6) rnds.

Set aside sts for sleeves as follows:
K29 (31, 38, 41), place next 46 (48, 53, 57) sts on a holder for sleeve, CO 7 sts for underarm, k61 (63, 79, 85), place next 46 (48, 53, 57) sts on a holder for sleeve, CO 7 sts for underarm, k29 (31, 38, 41) = 133 (139, 169, 181) sts rem for body.

With MC, work around until body measures 7½ (8¼, 9¾, 12¼) in [19 (21, 25, 31) cm]. Now work following chart B.
Knit 2 rnds with MC and, on the 2nd rnd, BO the 7 steek sts. Change to smaller-size circular and work back and forth in k1, p1 ribbing for 1⅜ in (3.5 cm). BO in ribbing on last row.

SLEEVES

With color A and larger-size dpn, CO 4 sts, knit the held 46 (48, 53, 57) sts, CO 3 sts = 53 (55, 60, 64) sts. The 1st (marked) st is always purled.

Work around for ¾ in (2 cm) and then begin shaping sleeve as follows:
Knit until 2 sts before marked purl st, sl, k1, psso, p1, k2tog.
Rep the decrease rnd every ⅝ in (1.5 cm) until 43 (43, 48, 54) sts rem.
Continue without further shaping until sleeve is 3½ (4¼, 6, 8¼) in [9 (11, 15, 21) cm] long. BO marked purl st on 2 largest sizes.

Work following chart B. Knit 1 rnd.
Knit 1 rnd, decreasing 4 (4, 6, 6) sts evenly spaced around = 38 (38, 42, 48) sts rem.
Change to smaller-size dpn and work around in k1, p1 ribbing for 1 (1¼, 1¼, 1¼) in [2.5 (3, 3, 3) cm]. BO in ribbing on last rnd.

Make 2nd sleeve the same way.

FINISHING

Machine-stitch 2 fine lines on each side of center steek st. Carefully cut steek up center st.

With color A (MC) and smaller-size circular, pick up an knit approx. 3 sts for every 4 rows along front edge. Work 8 rows in k1, p1 ribbing. BO in ribbing—make sure bind-off is not too tight.

On the boy's version, make the buttonholes on the left front band and on the right band for a girl. Make 6 (6, 7, 7) buttonholes evenly spaced on band.

Buttonhole: BO 2 sts on row 3; on row 4, CO 2 sts over each gap.

Fold cut edges down on WS and sew down with small stitches. If it is difficult to make a fine edge, you can knit a facing over the steek. Pick up and knit sts as you did for front bands. Work back and forth in stockinette until band is wide enough to cover cut edges. BO and sew facing over steek edges. So it won't show, sew down facings with MC.

Seam underarms. Sew down short lower ends of button bands. Sew on buttons. Weave in all ends neatly on WS.

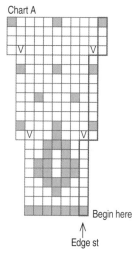

Chart A

Begin here

↑
Edge st

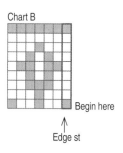

Chart B

Begin here

↑
Edge st

☐ Color A (MC)

▨ Color B

Ⓥ Increase here. Increase with M1: lift strand between 2 sts and knit into back loop with color A.

Winter Pine Cone Onesie in color A 1020, color B 4331, color C 1013.
Winter Pine Cone Pullover in color A 4331, color B 1013, color C 1020.
Winter Pine Cone Pants in color A 4331, color B 1013.

Little Winter Pine Cone Cap

A sweet cap knitted with fine yarn, with the simple winter pine cone pattern.
A knot at each side and good earflaps with ties on the smallest sizes all combine
to make a fine cap that will fit the wearer's head well.

SIZES: 0–2 (2–4, 4–9, 12, 18–24 months, 3–4, 5–6 years)

MATERIALS
YARN: Sandnes Garn KlompeLompe Tynn Merinoull (fine Merino wool) [CYCA #1 – fingering, 100% Merino wool, 191 yd (175 m) / 50 g]
YARN COLORS AND AMOUNTS:
Color A 4331 (MC): 50 (50, 50, 50, 50, 50, 50) g
Color B 1013: 50 (50, 50, 50, 50, 50, 50) g
NEEDLES: US sizes 1.5 and 2.5 (2.5 and 3 mm): 16 in (40 cm) circulars and sets of 5 dpn or use 32 in (80 cm) circular for magic loop (see video on magic loop technique on klompelompe.no).

GAUGE: 27 sts on larger-size needles = 4 in (10 cm).
Adjust needle size to obtain correct gauge if necessary.

The cap is worked in the round on a short circular, beginning at center back.

With smaller-size circular and color A (MC), CO 80 (88, 92, 96, 104, 112, 120) sts. Join, being careful not to twist cast-on row; pm for beginning of rnd.
  Work around in k1, p ribbing for 1¼ (1¼, 1¼, 1¼, 1½, 1½, 1½) in [3 (3, 3, 3, 4, 4, 4) cm].
  Change to larger-size circular.
Knit 2 rnds—on the 1st rnd, increase 4 (2, 4, 6, 4, 2, 0) sts evenly spaced around = 84 (90, 96, 102, 108, 114, 120) sts. Now work following chart until cap measures approx. 4½ (5¾, 6, 6½, 7¼, 7¾, 7¾) in [11.5 (14.5, 15.5, 16.5, 18.5, 19.5, 19.5) cm].

On the next rnd, BO all sts except for 10 sts centered at each side. Alternately, place the 10 sts at each side on a holder and later join the sets of sts with mattress st.

With dpn or magic loop circular, knit around on the 10 sts at 1 side for 4¾ in (12 cm). Cut yarn and draw through rem sts; tighten. Do the same on the 10 sts on opposite side.

If seaming sts, use mattress st (see page 124).

Earflaps for the smallest sizes:
There should be about 20 sts between the earflaps at center back. With color A and smaller-size needles, pick up and knit 18 (22, 22, 22, 24, 24, 0) sts. Work 3 rows in stockinette.
Decrease row (RS): K1, sl 1, k1, psso, knit until 3 sts rem k2tog, k1.
All WS Rows: Purl.

Rep these 2 rows until 4 sts rem. With rem 4 sts, knit an I-cord (see page 127) 7 in (18 cm) long.
Make 2nd earflap the same way.

FINISHING
Weave in all ends neatly on WS.
Place damp towel on cap and leave until completely dry.

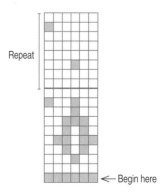

Repeat

← Begin here

Little Winter Pine Cone Socks

Knit a pair of socks to go with the other Winter Pine Cone garments and you'll have a pretty set for baby. The socks are sized for newborn to 3 years and are perfect for small, cold feet.

SIZES: 0–4 (4–12, 18 months, 2–3 years)

MATERIALS

YARN: Sandnes Garn KlompeLompe Tynn Merinoull (fine Merino wool) [CYCA #1 – fingering, 100% Merino wool, 191 yd (175 m) / 50 g]

YARN COLORS AND AMOUNTS:
Color 4032 (MC): 50 (50, 50, 50) g + small amount of contrast color

NEEDLES: US size 2.5 (3 mm): set of 5 dpn or use 32 in (80 cm) circular for magic loop (see video on magic loop technique on klompelompe.no).

GAUGE: 27 sts = 4 in (10 cm).
Adjust needle size to obtain correct gauge if necessary.

The socks are knitted in the round from the cuff down.

With MC, CO 40 (48, 48, 56) sts. Divide sts onto dpn and join. Work 5 rnds in k1, p1 ribbing.
     Knit 2 rnds.
     Now work in pattern following chart.

After working chart repeat 4 (4, 5, 5) times, end pattern. Continue with MC only.
     Knit 2 rnds, and, on 2nd rnd, decrease 0 (6, 2, 8) sts evenly spaced around = 40 (42, 46, 48) sts rem.

Make Eyelets:
Size 0–4 months: (K2tog, yo, k2) around.
Size 4–12 months: (K2tog, yo, k2) 5 times, k2, (k2tog, yo, k2) 5 times.
Size 18 months: (K2tog, yo, k2) 5 times, k6, (k2tog, yo, k2) 5 times.
Size 2–3 years: (K2tog, yo, k2) around.

Knit 3 rnds. Cut yarn.
     Place the 1st 12 (13, 14, 14) sts and last 12 (13, 14, 14) sts on a holder and work the center 16 (16, 18, 20) sts separately.

Front/Instep
Work back and forth in stockinette.
Work in stockinette for approx. 1⅜ (1¾, 2¼, 2½) in [3.5 (4.5, 5.5, 6.5) cm]
Next Row: K2tog, knit until 2 sts rem, sl 1, k1, psso.

Decrease the same way on every RS row a total of 3 (3, 4, 4) times and then BO on next, WS, row.

Begin again at center back where the round had begun previously.
     Knit 1st set of sts from the holder, pick up and knit 3 sts for every 4 rows across instep and then knit rem sts on holder = 62 (68, 74, 80) sts. Divide sts onto dpn and work around in garter st (= alternate knit and purl rnds).
     Work in garter st for 3.5 (3.5, 4.5, 5.5) ridges (2 rnds/rows = 1 ridge); the next row is knit.
     Decrease as follows:
Decrease Rnd 1: K1, k2tog, k22 (25, 28, 31), k2tog, k8, k2tog, k22 (25, 28, 31), k2tog, k1. Purl 1 rnd.
Decrease Rnd 2: K1, k2tog, k18 (21, 24, 27), k2tog, k2tog, k8, k2tog, k2tog, k18 (21, 24, 27), k2tog, k1.
Purl 1 rnd.
Decrease Rnd 3: K1, k2tog, k2tog, k17 (20, 23, 26), k2tog, k1, k2tog, k1, k2tog, k17 (20, 23, 26), k2tog, k2tog, k1.
Purl 1 rnd.
Decrease Rnd 4: K1, k2tog, k16 (19, 22, 25), k2tog, k3, k2tog, k16 (19, 22, 25), k2tog, k1.
Purl 1 rnd.

BO knitwise.

Seam sole of sock. Weave in all ends neatly
on WS. Make an I-cord and thread it through
eyelet rnd on sock.

Make 2nd sock the same way.
Place damp towel on socks and leave until
completely dry.

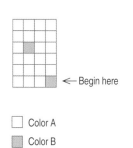

← Begin here

☐ Color A
▨ Color B

31

Little Winter Pine Cone Mittens

Mittens knit on fine needles with a fun two-color pattern.
Fabulous for anyone wanting to try stranded colorwork for the first time.

SIZES: 0–3 (3-6, 9–12 months, 1–2, 3–6, 8–12 years)

MATERIALS
YARN: Sandnes Garn KlompeLompe Tynn Merinoull (fine Merino wool) [CYCA #1 – fingering, 100% Merino wool, 191 yd (175 m) / 50 g]
YARN COLORS AND AMOUNTS:
Color A 1020 (MC): 50 (50, 50, 50, 50, 50) g
Color B 4344: 50 (50, 50, 50, 50, 50) g
Color C 1013: 50 (50, 50, 50, 50, 50) g
NEEDLES: US size 1.5 and 2.5 (2.5 and 3 mm): sets of 5 dpn or use 32 in (80 cm) circular for magic loop (see video on magic loop technique on klompelompe.no).

GAUGE: 27 sts on larger-size needles = 4 in (10 cm).
Adjust needle size to obtain correct gauge if necessary.

The round begins at the side.

With smaller-size dpn and color A (MC), CO 36 (40, 40, 44, 44, 44) sts. Divide sts onto dpn and join. Work 14 (14, 14, 16, 18, 18) rnds in k1, p1 ribbing.
    Work eyelets on next rnd as follows:
Size 0–3 months: (K1, p1, k2tog, yo) 2 times, k1, p1, k1, p1, (k1, p1, k2tog, yo) 6 times.
Size 3–6 and 9–12 months: (K1, p1, k2tog, yo) around.
Size 1–2, 3–6, 8–12 years: (K1, p1, k2tog, yo) 2 times, k1, p1, k1, p1, (k1, p1, k2tog, yo) 8 times.
All sizes: Work 3 rnds in k1, p1 ribbing.

Change to larger-size dpn.
    Knit 1 rnd, increasing 0 (2, 8, 10, 10, 10) sts evenly spaced around = 36 (42, 48, 54, 54, 54) sts.
    Knit 2 rnds and then work following charted pattern. Pm at each side = 18 (21, 24, 27, 27, 27) sts on each side.

Sizes 1–2, 3–6, 8–12 years: When piece measures 3¼ (3½, 4¾) in [8 (9, 12) cm], make a thumb as follows:

LEFT-HAND MITTEN
Work across front, knit 18 (17 16) sts in pattern, knit the next 7 (8, 9) sts with smooth contrast color waste yarn, slide the 7 (8, 9) sts back to left needle, and work 9 (10, 11) sts in pattern.

RIGHT-HAND MITTEN
Work across front, knit 2 sts in pattern, knit the next 7 (8, 9) sts with smooth contrast color waste yarn, slide the 7 (8, 9) sts back to left needle and work 25 sts in pattern.

When piece measures approx. 3½ (4¼, 4¾, 5½, 6¼, 7¼) in [9 (11, 12, 14, 16, 18.5) cm], continuing in pattern, shape mitten top as follows:
*K1, k2tog, knit until 2 sts before marker, sl 1,

k1, psso *; rep * to * once more.
    Decrease the same way on every rnd until 8 (10, 10, 10, 10, 10) sts rem. Cut yarn and draw end through rem sts; tighten.

THUMB
Insert a dpn into the 7 (8, 9) sts below waste yarn and another dpn into the 7 (8, 9) sts above waste yarn. Carefully remove waste yarn.
    With color A, knit around until thumb measures 1½ (2, 2½) in / [4 (5, 6) cm]. K2tog around = 7 (8, 9) sts rem. Cut yarn and draw end through rem sts; tighten.

FINISHING
Weave in all ends neatly on WS.
Place damp towel on mittens and leave until completely dry.
Make 2 I-cords with color B and thread through eyelet rounds.

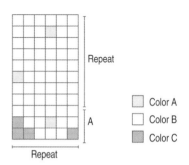

Golden Summer Cap color 4344
Winter Pine Cone Pants with color A
4331, color B 1013

Easter

Easter Pullover for Women

SIZES: XS–S (M, L, XL)

FINISHED MEASUREMENTS

Chest: Approx. 35 (37, 42¼, 46½) in [89 (94, 107, 118) cm]

Total Length: Approx. 22½ (23¼, 24¾, 25½) in [57 (59, 63, 65) cm]

MATERIALS

YARN: Sandnes Garn KlompeLompe Spøt [CYCA #3 – DK, light worsted, 40% Merino wool, 40% alpaca, 20% nylon, 147 yd (134 m) / 50 g] [this yarn has been discontinued]

YARN COLORS AND AMOUNTS:

Color 1013: 350 (450, 500, 550) g

NEEDLES: US sizes 2.5 and 4 (3 and 3.5 mm): 16 and 24 in (40 and 60 cm) circulars and sets of 5 dpn or use 32 in (80 cm) circular for magic loop (see video on magic loop technique on klompelompe.no).

GAUGE: 22 sts on larger-size needles = 4 in (10 cm).

Adjust needle size to obtain correct gauge if necessary.

The pullover begins with the sleeves worked on either dpn or long magic loop circular.

SLEEVES

With smaller size dpn or magic loop circular, CO 46 (46, 48, 50) sts. Divide sts onto dpn and join. Work around in k1, p1 ribbing for 3¼ in (8 cm).

Change to larger-size needles. Always purl the 1st (marked) st for center of underarm.

Knit 1 rnd.

On next rnd, pm as follows:

P1, k13 (13, 14, 15), pm, work 19 sts in pattern, pm, k13 (13, 14, 15).

Continue in stockinette, with pattern over the 19 sts between markers.

PATTERN

Rnd 1: P1, k17, p1.
Rnd 2: P1, k17, p1.
Rnd 3: P1, k1, knot, k3, knot, k3, knot, k1, p1.
Rnds 4–6: P1, k17, p1.
Rnd 7: P1, k4, knot, k3, knot, k3, k1, p1.
Rnd 8: P1, k17, p1.

KNOT

P3tog, leave sts on left needle, knit the same 3 sts tog, and then p3tog again. Slip sts off left needle.

Work around as est for ¾ in (2 cm). Now begin shaping sleeve as follows:

P1, M1, work rnd end of rnd, M1.

Increase the same way every 1⅜ (1⅜, 1, 1) in [3.5 (3.5, 2.5, 2.5) cm] to 72 (76, 80, 82) sts.

Continue without further shaping until sleeve is 19 in (48 cm) long or desired length.

BO 9 sts centered on underarm. Set sleeve aside and make 2nd sleeve the same way.

BODY

With smaller-size circular, CO 196 (206, 236, 260) sts, Join, being careful not to twist cast-on row; pm for beginning of rnd and at side [= 98 (103, 118, 130) sts each for front and back]. Work around in k1, p1 ribbing for 3¼ in (8 cm).

The rnd begins at the side.

Change to larger-size circular and knit around until body measures 15½ (15½, 15¾, 15¾) in [39 (39, 40, 40) cm].

On next rnd, BO 9 sts centered at each side for underarms.

YOKE

Now join the sleeves and body. Don't forget to continue the 19 pattern sts on each sleeve.

Begin at left sleeve, then work front, right sleeve, and back = 304 (322, 360, 388) sts total. Pm at each intersection of body and sleeve = 4 raglan markers. Knit 3 rnds.

Begin decreasing on next rnd: *K1, sl 1, k1, psso, work until 3 sts before next raglan marker, k2tog, k1*; rep * to * around = 8 sts decreased.

Decrease the same way on every other round a total of 6 (6, 7, 7) times = 256 (274, 304, 332) sts rem.

Remove raglan markers. Rnd now begins at center back.

Work 2 rnds without decreasing.

On next rnd, decrease as follows:

Work until 1 st before pattern section, p2tog, work 17 sts in pattern, p2tog; rep * to * in other pattern section = 4 sts decreased.

Work 3 rnds without decreasing.

Work 1 rnd, decreasing 4 sts as above. Work 3 rnds without decreasing.

Work 1 rnd, decreasing 4 sts as above. Work 2 rnds without decreasing.

Work 1 rnd, decreasing 4 sts as above. Work 2 rnds without decreasing.

Work 1 rnd, decreasing 4 sts as above.

Work 1 rnd without decreasing.
Now decrease the same way on every rnd until 108 (114,120, 124) sts rem.

Knit 1 rnd and decrease 13 (14, 20, 24) sts evenly spaced around.

NECKBAND
Work around in k2, p3 ribbing for 8 in (20 cm) and then BO in ribbing. Make sure the bind-off is not too tight.

FINISHING
Seam underarms. Weave in all ends neatly on WS.
Lay a damp towel over pullover and leave until completely dry. You can also steam-press the sweater under a damp pressing cloth, but make sure you don't press too hard on the pattern section.

Easter Pullover for Men

We put a new twist on the neck shaping for
this pullover. It's an exciting knitting project
and, at the same time, very easy.

SIZES: S (M, L, XL)

FINISHED MEASUREMENTS

Chest: Approx. 36¾ (39, 42¼, 45¼) in [93 (99, 107, 115) cm]

Total Length: Approx. 27½ (29¼, 30, 30¾) in [70 (74.5, 76, 78) cm]

MATERIALS

YARN: Sandnes Garn KlompeLompe Spøt [CYCA #3 – DK, light worsted, 40% Merino wool, 40% alpaca, 20% nylon, 147 yd (134 m) / 50 g]

YARN COLORS AND AMOUNTS:

Color 7251: 500 (550, 650, 700) g

NEEDLES: US sizes 2.5 and 4 (3 and 3.5 mm): 16 and 24 in (40 and 60 cm) circulars and sets of 5 dpn or use 32 in (80 cm) circular for magic loop (see video on magic loop technique on klompelompe.no).

GAUGE: 22 sts on larger-size needles = 4 in (10 cm).

Adjust needle size to obtain correct gauge if necessary.

• •

The pullover begins with the sleeves worked on either dpn or long magic loop circular.

SLEEVES

With smaller-size dpn or magic loop circular, CO 52 (56, 62, 64) sts. Divide sts onto dpn and join. Work around in k1, p1 ribbing for 3¼ in (8 cm).

Change to larger-size needles. Always purl the 1st (marked) st for center of under-arm.

Knit 1 rnd.

On next rnd, pm as follows:

P1, k16 (18, 21, 22), pm, work 19 sts in pattern, pm, k16 (18, 21, 22).

Continue in stockinette, with pattern over the 19 sts between markers.

PATTERN

Rnds 1–2: *P1, k1*; rep * to * until 1 st rem, end p1.

Rnd 3: Knit around.

Rnd 4: Purl around.

Work around as est for ¾ in (2 cm). Now begin shaping sleeve as follows:

P1, M1, work rnd end of rnd, M1.

Increase the same way every ¾ in (2 cm) to 94 (98, 102, 108) sts.

Continue without further shaping until sleeve is 20½ in (52 cm) long or desired length.

BO 9 sts centered on underarm. Set sleeve aside and make 2nd sleeve the same way.

BODY

With smaller-size circular, CO 204 (218, 236, 252) sts. Join, being careful not to twist cast-on row; pm for beginning of rnd and at side [= 102 (109, 118, 126) sts each for front and back]. Work around in k1, p1 ribbing for 3¼ in (8 cm).

The rnd begins at the side.

Change to larger-size circular and knit around until body measures 19 (19¼, 19¾, 20) in [48 (49, 50, 51) cm].

On next rnd, BO 9 sts centered at each side.

YOKE

Now join the sleeves and body. Don't forget to continue the 19 pattern sts on each sleeve.

Begin at left sleeve, then work front, right sleeve, and back = 356 (378, 404, 432) sts total. Pm at each intersection of body and sleeve = 4 raglan marker. Knit 3 rnds.

Begin decreasing on next rnd: *K1, sl 1, k1, psso, work until 3 sts before next raglan marker, k2tog, k1*; rep * to * around = 8 sts decreased.

Decrease the same way on every other round a total of 9 (10, 11, 11) times = 284 (298, 316, 344) sts rem.

Remove raglan markers. Rnd now begins at center back.

Work 2 rnds without decreasing.

On next rnd, decrease as follows:

Work until 1 st before pattern section, p2tog (if you are on Rnd 3 of pattern, k2tog), work 17 sts in pattern, p2tog (if you are on Rnd 3 of pattern, k2tog tbl); rep * to * in other pattern section = 4 sts decreased.

Work 3 rnds without decreasing.

Work 1 rnd, decreasing 4 sts as above. Work 3 rnds without decreasing.

Work 1 rnd, decreasing 4 sts as above. Work 2 rnds without decreasing.

Work 1 rnd, decreasing 4 sts as above. Work 2 rnds without decreasing.

Work 1 rnd, decreasing 4 sts as above. Work 1 rnd without decreasing.

Now decrease the same way on every rnd until 120 (118,132, 132) sts rem.

Knit 1 rnd and decrease 20 (18, 22, 22) sts evenly spaced around.

NECKBAND

Work around in k2, p3 ribbing for 8 in (20 cm) and then BO in ribbing. Make sure the bind-off is not too tight.

FINISHING

Seam underarms. Weave in all ends neatly on WS.

Lay a damp towel over pullover and leave until completely dry. You can also steam-press the sweater under a damp pressing cloth, but make sure you don't press too hard on the pattern section.

Easter Pullover for Children

The high neck and soft yarn make this the perfect pullover for mountain hikes or an egg hunt in the woods. You can choose either a texture or knot pattern for the sleeves.

SIZES: 1 (2, 4, 6, 8, 10, 12, 14) years

FINISHED MEASUREMENTS
Chest: Approx. 22¾ (23¾, 24¾, 25¾, 28¼, 30¼, 32¼, 34¼) in [58 (60, 63, 65.5, 72, 77, 82, 87) cm]
Total Length: Approx. 13¾ (15, 16½, 17¾, 20, 22, 22¾, 24) in [35 (38, 42, 45, 51, 56, 58, 61) cm] + yoke

MATERIALS
YARN: Sandnes Garn KlompeLompe Spøt [CYCA #3 – DK, light worsted, 40% Merino wool, 40% alpaca, 20% nylon, 147 yd (134 m) / 50 g]
YARN COLORS AND AMOUNTS:
Color 4032 or 7251: 200 (200, 250, 250, 300, 350, 350, 400) g
NEEDLES: US sizes 2.5 and 4 (3 and 3.5 mm): 16 and 24 in (40 and 60 cm) circulars and sets of 5 dpn or use 32 in (80 cm) circular for magic loop (see video on magic loop technique on klompelompe.no).

GAUGE: 22 sts on larger-size needles = 4 in (10 cm).
Adjust needle size to obtain correct gauge if necessary.

The pullover begins with the sleeves worked on either dpn or long magic loop circular.

SLEEVES
With smaller-size dpn or magic loop circular, CO 36 (36, 38, 38, 40, 40, 42, 42) sts. Divide sts onto dpn and join. Work around in k1, p1 ribbing for 1½ in (4 cm).

Change to larger-size needles. Always purl the 1st (marked) st for center of under-arm.

Knit 1 rnd.
On next rnd, pm as follows:
P1, k8 (8, 9, 9, 10, 10, 11, 11), pm, work 19 sts in pattern, pm, k8 (8, 9, 9, 10, 10, 11, 11).

Continue in stockinette, with pattern over the 19 sts between markers.

PATTERN WITH KNOTS
Rnd 1: P1, k17, p1.
Rnd 2: P1, k17, p1.
Rnd 3: P1, k1, knot, k3, knot, k3, knot, k1, p1.
Rnds 4–6: P1, k17, p1.
Rnd 7: P1, k4, knot, k3, knot, k3, k1, p1.
Rnd 8: P1, k17, p1.

KNOT
P3tog, leave sts on left needle, knit the same 3 sts tog, and then p3tog again. Slip sts off left needle.

PATTERN WITH KNIT/PURL TEXTURE
Rnds 1–2: *P1, k1*; rep * to * until 1 st rem, end p1.
Rnd 3: Knit around.
Rnd 4: Purl around.

Work around as est for ¾ in (2 cm). Now begin shaping sleeve as follows:
P1, M1, work rnd end of rnd, M1.
Increase the same way every 1¼ in (3 cm) to 48 (50, 52, 54, 58, 62, 66, 70) sts.
Continue without further shaping until sleeve is 9½ (11, 12¼, 13, 14 ¼, 15, 15¾, 16) in [24 (28, 31, 34, 36, 38, 40, 42) cm] long or desired length.
BO 7 sts centered on underarm. Set sleeve aside and make 2nd sleeve the same way.

BODY
With smaller-size circular, CO 128 (132, 138, 144, 158, 170, 180, 192) sts, Join, being careful not to twist cast-on row; pm for begin-ning of rnd and at side [= 64 (66, 69, 72, 79, 85, 90, 96) sts each for front and back]. Work around in k1, p1 ribbing for 1½ in (4 cm).
The rnd begins at the side.
Change to larger-size circular and knit around until body measures 8¼ (9½, 10¼, 11¾, 13, 14¼, 15, 15½) in [21 (24, 26, 30, 33, 36, 38, 39) cm].
On next rnd, BO 7 sts centered at each side for underarms.

Color 1013

YOKE

Now join the sleeves and body. Don't forget to continue the 19 pattern sts on each sleeve.

Begin at left sleeve, then work front, right sleeve, and back = 196 (204, 214, 224, 246, 266, 284, 304) sts total. Pm at each intersection of body and sleeve = 4 raglan markers. Knit 3 rnds.

Begin decreasing on next rnd: *K1, sl 1, k1, psso, work until 3 sts before next raglan marker, k2tog, k1*; rep * to * around = 8 sts decreased.

Decrease the same way on every other round a total of 2 (3, 3, 3, 4, 4, 4, 4) times = 180 (180, 190, 200, 214, 234, 252, 272) sts rem.

Remove raglan markers. Rnd now begins at center back.

Work 3 (3, 3, 3, 4, 4, 4, 5) rnds without decreasing.

On next rnd, decrease as follows:

Work until 1 st before pattern section, p2tog, work 17 sts in pattern, p2tog; rep * to * in other pattern section = 4 sts decreased. **Note** If you are working knit/purl texture pattern on sleeves, and if you are on Rnd 3 of pattern, k2tog instead of p2tog.

Work 3 rnds without decreasing.

Work 1 rnd, decreasing 4 sts as above. Work 3 rnds without decreasing.

Work 1 rnd, decreasing 4 sts as above. Work 2 rnds without decreasing.

Work 1 rnd, decreasing 4 sts as above. Work 2 rnds without decreasing.

Work 1 rnd, decreasing 4 sts as above. Work 1 rnd without decreasing.

Now decrease the same way on every rnd until 80 (80, 90, 92, 92, 90, 96, 98) sts rem. Knit 1 rnd and decrease 0 (0, 0, 2, 2, 0, 1, 3) sts evenly spaced around.

NECKBAND

Work around in k2, p3 ribbing for 4 (4, 4, 4, 4¾, 4¾, 5½, 5½) in [10 (10, 10, 10, 12, 12, 14, 14) cm] and then BO in ribbing. Make sure the bind-off is not too tight.

FINISHING

Seam underarms. Weave in all ends neatly on WS.

Lay a damp towel over pullover and leave until completely dry. You can also steampress the sweater under a damp pressing cloth, but make sure you don't press too hard on the pattern section.

Billebæ Cap

Our new favorite! A perfectly fitting cap with the sweetest look.
You can decide if you want short or long ears. The cap is knitted with
two strands held together. The distinctive ridges make it nice and cozy.

SIZES: 6–12 months (1–2, 3–4, 5–6) years

MATERIALS

YARN: Sandnes Garn KlompeLompe Merinoull (Merino wool) [CYCA #3 – DK, light worsted, 100% Merino wool, 114 yd (104 m) / 50 g]
Sandnes Garn KlompeLompe Tynn Merinoull (fine Merino wool) [CYCA #1 – fingering, 100% Merino wool, 191 yd (175 m) / 50 g]

YARN COLORS AND AMOUNTS:
Cap with short ears:
Color 2652:
Merinoull: 100 (100, 100, 150) g
Tynn Merinoull: 50 (50, 50, 50) g
Cap with long ears:
Color 2652:
Merinoull: 100 (100, 150, 150) g
Tynn Merinoull: 50 (50, 50, 50) g

NEEDLES: US sizes 6 and 8 (4 and 5 mm): 16 and 24 in (40 and 60 cm) circulars and sets of 5 dpn

GAUGE: 16 sts on larger-size needles = 4 in (10 cm).
Adjust needle size to obtain correct gauge if necessary.

The cap begins at the lower edge and is worked in the round on a circular needle with a strand of each yarn held together.

With larger-size circular and both yarns held together, CO 104 (104, 112, 120) sts. Join, being careful not to twist cast-on row; pm for beginning of rnd. Purl 2 rnds. Knit the next rnd, placing a marker after 22 (22, 24, 26), 30 (30, 32, 34), 22 (22, 24, 26), 30 (30, 32, 34) sts = 4 markers.

Knit 1 rnd, decreasing as follows: *K2tog, knit until 2 sts before marker, sl 1, k1, psso. Rep from * around = 8 sts decreased.

Now work in pattern: *Purl 2 rnds, k 2 rnds.*

At the same time, decrease the same way on *every* knit rnd, a total of 8 (8, 8, 9) times = 40 (40, 48, 48) sts rem. **Note** You will decrease on 2 rnds in a row and then work 2 rnds without decreasing.

Knit 1 rnd, purl 2 rnds (on the largest size, work only 2 purl rnds).

Work in k1, p1 ribbing for 1⅝ (1¾, 2, 2) in [4 (4.5, 5, 5) cm]. Do not work ribbing too tightly.

Next rnd: Rib 11 (11, 13, 13) sts, slip 6 (6, 8, 8) sts to a holder, work 23 (23, 27, 27) sts in ribbing.

Cut yarn and place the 1st 11 (11, 13, 13) sts on same needle as last sts.
Work back and forth on these 34 (34, 40, 40) sts from now on, leaving rem 6 (6, 8, 8) sts on holder.

The 1st row is RS. Pm at center back.
Now work in pattern:

Row 1 (RS): Purl.
Row 2 (WS): Knit.
Row 3 (RS): Knit.
Row 4 (WS): Purl.

Work 2 rows.

Read the next section of instructions before you begin knitting.

K2tog at beginning and end of every other row, 2 times = 4 sts decreased = 30 (30, 36, 36) sts rem.

At the same time, increase for back of head on every other row (RS) as follows:

Work until 1 st before marker, increase with M1 with knit or purl depending on pattern row, work 1 st after marker, M1. Increase a total of 7 (8, 8, 9) times = 14 (16, 16, 18) sts increased = 44 (46, 52, 54) sts.

Continue in pattern until head measures 5¼ (5½, 5½, 6) in [13 (14, 14, 15) cm] from end of ribbing. Do not stretch cap while measuring.

Increase 1 st at beginning and end of row with kf&b or pf&b (depending on pattern). Increase the same way on every other row a total of 2 times = 4 sts increased = 48 (50, 56, 58) sts.

Continue in pattern until piece measures 6¾ (7, 7½, 8) in [17 (18, 19, 20) cm] from ribbing and you've just purled a row on RS.

Now turn the piece with the wrong side out so the beginning and end of the row meet and you can knit them together with 3-needle bind-off: K2tog joining 1st st of front needle and 1st st of back needle, *k2tog, pass 1st st on right needle over 2nd to bind off; rep from * to end. After joining all sts, turn cap right side out.

Now work the ribbing around the face. Use smaller-size needle and a single strand of Merinoull. Work 1st 6 (6, 8, 8) sts from holder and then pick up and knit 74 (78, 80, 84) sts = 80 (84, 88, 92) sts total. Work in the round in k1, p1 ribbing for 1¼ (1¼, 1⅜, 1⅜) in [3 (3, 3.5, 3.5) cm] and then BO, making sure bind-off is neither too tight nor too loose. The cap should fit well around the face.

EARS

With smaller-size dpn and a single strand of Merinoull, CO 40 sts. Divide sts onto dpn or magic loop circular (for magic loop, see video on technique at klompelompe.no) and join. Knit around in stockinette for 2½ in (6 cm) for short ears or 5½ in (14 cm) for long ears.

Decrease Rnd 1: (K2, k2tog) around.
Knit 1 rnd.
Decrease Rnd 2 (K1, k2tog) around.
Knit 1 rnd.
Decrease Rnd 3: (K2tog) around.
Decrease Rnd 4: (K2tog) around.

FINISHING
Cut yarn. Draw end through rem sts and tighten.

Fold each ear lengthwise and sew down securely to a garter st rnd. Sew ear about 1½ in (4 cm) from ribbing around face and s4 (4, 5, 5) ridges from the top.

Weave in all ends neatly on WS. Lay a damp towel over cap and leave until dry or gently steam-press cap under a damp pressing cloth.

Golden Summer Cap

A summer cap with the same fine structure pattern
as on the Golden Summer Rompers.

SIZES: 0–1 months (3, 6–9 months, 1–2, 3–6,
8–12) years

MATERIALS

YARN: Sandnes Garn KlompeLompe
Merinoull (Merino wool) [CYCA #3 – DK, light
worsted, 100% Merino wool, 114 yd (104 m)
/ 50 g]

YARN COLORS AND AMOUNTS:

Color 4344: 50 (50, 50, 50, 100, 100) g

NEEDLES: US sizes 2.5 and 4 (3 and 3.5 mm):
16 in (40 cm) circulars and sets of 5 dpn;
optional 32 in (80 cm) circulars for magic
loop (for magic loop, see video on technique
at klompelompe.no)

NOTIONS: 2 decorative buttons

GAUGE: 22 sts on larger-size needles = 4 in
(10 cm).
Adjust needle size to obtain correct gauge
if necessary.

	◫	O				
			O			

☐ knit

⊡ yarnover

◨ k2tog tbl

With smaller-size circular, CO 68 (72, 76, 84,
92, 92) sts. Join, being careful not to twist
cast-on row; pm for beginning of rnd. Work
10 (10, 10, 13, 13, 13) rnds in pattern ribbing
below.

PATTERN RIBBING

Rnds 1–2: *K1tbl, p1*; rep * to * around.
Rnd 3: *Yo, k1tbl, p1, k1tbl, slip yarnover
over the 3 sts, p1*; rep * to * around.

Change to larger-size circular. Knit 1 rnd.
   Knit 1 rnd, increasing 4 (12, 20, 12, 16,
16) sts evenly spaced around = 72 (84, 96,
96, 108, 108) sts.
   Work in pattern following chart until cap
measures approx. 4 (4¼, 5¼, 6, 6¼, 7) in [10
(11, 13, 15, 16, 18) cm].

Now work around in stockinette, shaping
crown as follows:
Decrease Rnd 1: *K10, k2tog*; rep * to *
around.
Knit 1 rnd.
Decrease Rnd 2: *K9, k2tog*; rep * to *
around.
Knit 1 rnd.
Decrease Rnd 3: *K8, k2tog*; rep * to *
around.
Knit 1 rnd.
Decrease Rnd 4: *K7, k2tog*; rep * to *
around.
Knit 1 rnd.

Decrease Rnd 5: *K6, k2tog*; rep * to *
around.
Knit 1 rnd.
Decrease Rnd 6: *K5, k2tog*; rep * to *
around.
Knit 1 rnd.
Decrease Rnd 7: *K4, k2tog*; rep * to *
around.
Knit 1 rnd.
Decrease Rnd 8: *K3, k2tog*; rep * to *
around.
Decrease Rnd 9: *K2, k2tog*; rep * to *
around.
Decrease Rnd 10: *K1, k2tog*; rep * to *
around.
Decrease Rnd 11: *K2tog*; rep * to *
around.

Knit the rem 6 (7, 8, 8, 9, 9) sts for ¾ in (2
cm). Cut yarn, draw end through rem sts and
tighten.

FINISHING

Weave in all ends neatly on WS. Sew on
2 buttons. Lay a damp towel over cap and
leave until dry or gently steam-press cap
under a damp pressing cloth.

Golden Summer Rompers

Sweet rompers for the littlest ones featuring an unusual detail on the straps. We offer two versions of these rompers, with or without the lace pattern.

SIZES: 0–1 (3, 6, 9, 12, 18) months

FINISHED MEASUREMENTS:
Chest: Approx. 19¼ (19¼, 21, 21, 22, 22) in [49 (49, 53, 53, 56, 56) cm]
Total length excluding straps: Approx. 9½ (10¼, 11, 11¾, 12¾, 13½) in [24 (26, 28, 30, 32, 34) cm]

MATERIALS
YARN: Sandnes Garn Merinoull (Merino wool) [CYCA #3 – DK, light worsted, 100% Merino wool, 114 yd (104 m) / 50 g]
YARN COLORS AND AMOUNTS:
Color 1042: 100 (100, 100, 150, 150, 150) g
NEEDLES: US sizes 2.5 and 4 (3 and 3.5 mm): 16 in (40 cm) circulars and sets of 5 dpn
CROCHET HOOK: US size D-3 (3 mm)
NOTIONS: 6 buttons

GAUGE: 22 sts on larger-size needles = 4 in (10 cm).
Adjust needle size to obtain correct gauge if necessary.

The rompers are worked top down, in the round on circular needles.

With smaller-size circular, CO 108 (108, 116, 116, 124, 124) sts. Join, being careful not to twist cast-on row; pm for beginning of rnd.

Pattern Ribbing
Rnds 1–2: *K1tbl, p1*; rep * to * around.
Rnd 3: *Yo, k1tbl, p1, k1tbl, slip yarnover over the 3 sts, p1*; rep * to * around.

Work 16 (16, 16, 16, 19, 19) rnds in pattern ribbing below.

Note On the 7th rnd, make 2 buttonholes on the front:
Work 43 (43, 46, 46, 48, 48) sts in ribbing, BO 2 sts, work 18 (18, 20, 20, 24, 24) sts in ribbing, BO 2 sts, work 43 (43, 46, 46, 48, 48) sts in ribbing.
On the next rnd, CO 2 new sts over each gap.

Change to larger-size circular and knit 1 rnd. Knit 0 (0, 1, 1, 1, 1) rnd, increasing 0 (0, 4, 4, 2, 2) sts evenly spaced around = 108 (108, 120, 120, 126, 126) sts. Now work either in lace pattern following chart or in stockinette.

When piece measures approx. 6½ (7¼, 8¼, 9, 9½, 10¾) in [16.5 (18.5, 21, 23, 24, 27) cm], and you have just worked rnd 1 or 4 of chart, decrease at the sides as follows:

K24 (24, 25, 25, 26, 26), BO 12 (12, 16, 16, 17, 17) sts, k36 (36, 38, 38, 40, 40), BO 12 (12, 16, 16, 17, 17) sts, k24 (24, 25, 25, 26, 26).

Cut yarn. Place all sts for back on 1 needle and slide all front sts to another needle.

BACK
The 1st row is WS.
On every RS row, decrease 1 st at each side: k2tog at beginning of row and k2tog at end of row. Decrease the same way on every RS row until 22 sts rem. On next, WS, row, BO all sts purlwise.

FRONT
Work as for back but leave rem 22 sts on a holder.

With smaller-size circular, pick up and knit an odd number of sts around 1 leg opening, picking up 3 sts for every 4 sts/rows.

Work 3 rows back and forth in twisted rib;
WS: P1tbl, k1.
RS: K1tbl, p1.
Row 4: BO in ribbing.
Work 2nd leg band the same way.

BUTTON BANDS ON FRONT

With smaller-size circular, pick and knit 3 sts on end of ribbing on left leg, knit the held sts, pick up and knit 3 sts on end of ribbing around right leg.

Work 6 rows in ribbing, but, on row 2, make 4 buttonholes evenly spaced across: buttonhole = k2tog, yo.

Note: Do not make a button band on the back. The buttons are sewn directly onto the back.

STRAPS

With smaller-size circular, pick and knit 4 sts on back of romper, about 4 in (10 cm) from center back. Knit an I-cord (see page 127) 8¾ (8¾, 9½, 10¼, 10¼, 11) in [22 (22, 24, 26, 26, 28) cm] long. BO, leaving last st on needle. Chain 5 and attach to 1st chain to make a button loop.

Make another strap the same way. Cross the straps in the back. Sew a button about 2½ in (6 cm) from the end of each strap.

If desired, you can crank out the I-cords on a knitting mill and sew them securely to the back of the rompers with mattress st.

FINISHING

Weave in all ends neatly on WS. Sew 4 buttons to lower edge of back. Lay a damp towel over rompers and leave until dry or gently steam-press under a damp pressing cloth.

☐ knit on RS, purl on WS

O yo

◣ k2tog tbl on RS, p2tog tbl on WS

≪———— Colors, from left: 1042, 4331, 7251, 4032, 1013

Little Crafty Cap

A fun cap with spiraling bands of texture. An amusing and simple project. Make one in your favorite color.

SIZES: 6–9 months (1–2, 3–6, 8–14 years)

MATERIALS

YARN: Sandnes Garn KlompeLompe Merinoull (Merino wool) [CYCA #3 – DK, light worsted, 100% Merino wool, 114 yd (104 m) / 50 g]

YARN COLORS AND AMOUNTS:
Color 6061: 50 (50, 50, 100) g

NEEDLES: U.S. sizes 4 and 6 (3.5 and 4 mm): 16 in (40 cm) circulars and sets of 5 dpn

NOTIONS: 2 decorative buttons or small leather patch

GAUGE: 22 sts on larger-size needles = 4 in (10 cm).
Adjust needle size to obtain correct gauge if necessary.

The cap is knitted in the round.

With smaller-size circular, CO 72 (80, 80, 88) sts. Join, being careful not to twist cast-on row; pm for beginning of rnd.

  Work around in k1, p1 ribbing for 1 in (2.5 cm). Change to larger-size circular and knit 1 rnd, increasing 8 sts evenly spaced around. Now work following chart.

When cap measures 5¼ (5½, 6, 6¼) in [13 (14, 15, 16) cm], begin shaping crown (change to dpn when sts no longer fit around circular). Continue pattern as you shape crown.

Decrease Rnd 1: Decrease 1 st in each knit band with k2tog in the center 2 knit sts = 3 sts rem in each knit band.
Work 3 rnds in pattern.

Decrease Rnd 2: Decrease 1 st in each purl band with p2tog in the center 2 purl sts = 3 sts rem in each purl band.
Work 3 rnds in pattern.

Decrease Rnd 3: Decrease 1 st in each knit band with k2tog in the 1st 2 knit sts = 2 sts rem in each knit band.
Work 3 rnds in pattern.

Decrease Rnd 4: Decrease 1 st in each purl band with p2tog in the 1st 2 purl sts = 2 sts rem in each purl band.
Work 1 rnd in pattern.

Decrease Rnd 5: Decrease 1 st in each knit band with k2tog = 1 st rem in each knit band.
Work 1 rnd in pattern.

Decrease Rnd 6: Decrease 1 st in each purl band with p2tog = 1 st rem in each purl band.

Last decrease rnd: K2tog around.

FINISHING

Cut yarn and draw end through rem sts; tighten. Weave in all ends neatly on WS. Sew on 2 buttons or a leather patch. Lay a damp towel over cap and leave until dry or gently steam-press cap under a damp pressing cloth.

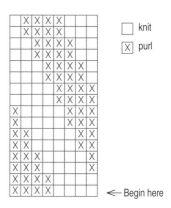

☐ knit
☒ purl

← Begin here

Theodor pullover, color A 1013, color B 6061.

If you know how to knit and purl, then this cowl is perfect for you. A super project for a beginner knitter.

Crafty Cowl for Adults

Little Crafty Cowl

SIZES: Women's (Men's)

MATERIALS

YARN: Sandnes Garn KlompeLompe Merinoull (Merino wool) [CYCA #3 – DK, light worsted, 100% Merino wool, 114 yd (104 m) / 50 g]

YARN COLORS AND AMOUNTS:
Color 1013 (6061): 250 (150) g

NEEDLES: U.S. size 6 (4 mm): 16 in (40 cm) circular

GAUGE: 22 sts on larger-size needles = 4 in (10 cm).
Adjust needle size to obtain correct gauge if necessary.

CO 140 (130) sts. Join, being careful not to twist cast-on row; pm for beginning of rnd.

Work around in k1, p1 ribbing for 6 rnds and then work following chart.

When cowl measures approx. 21¾ (11¾) in [55 (30) cm], work 6 rnds in k1, p1 ribbing. BO in ribbing.

FINISHING
Weave in all ends neatly on WS. Lay a damp towel over cowl and leave until completely dry.

SIZES: Child

MATERIALS

YARN: Sandnes Garn KlompeLompe Merinoull (Merino wool) [CYCA #3 – DK, light worsted, 100% Merino wool, 114 yd (104 m) / 50 g]

YARN COLORS AND AMOUNTS:
Color 7251: 100 g

NEEDLES: U.S. size 6 (4 mm): 16 in (40 cm) circular

GAUGE: 22 sts on larger-size needles = 4 in (10 cm).
Adjust needle size to obtain correct gauge if necessary.

CO 112 sts. Join, being careful not to twist cast-on row; pm for beginning of rnd.

Work around in k1, p1 ribbing for 6 rnds and then work following chart.

When cowl measures approx. 9¾ in (25) cm], work 6 rnds in k1, p1 ribbing. BO in ribbing.

FINISHING
Weave in all ends neatly on WS. Lay a damp towel over cowl and leave until completely dry.

Adult

□ knit
X purl

Begin here

Child

← Begin here

Large Crafty Cap

Here's a quick project. The pattern is easy and you can personalize it. Embellish it with leather patch or a couple of buttons.

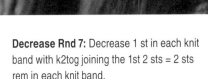

SIZES: Women's (Men's)

MATERIALS

YARN: Sandnes Garn KlompeLompe Merinoull (Merino wool) [CYCA #3 – DK, light worsted, 100% Merino wool, 114 yd (104 m) / 50 g]

YARN COLORS AND AMOUNTS:
Color 4344 (6571): 100 (100) g

NEEDLES: U.S. sizes 4 and 6 (3.5 and 4 mm): 16 in (40 cm) circulars and sets of 5 dpn

NOTIONS: 2 decorative buttons or small leather patch

GAUGE: 22 sts on larger-size needles = 4 in (10 cm).
Adjust needle size to obtain correct gauge if necessary.

The cap is knitted in the round.

With smaller-size circular, CO 88 (92) sts. Join, being careful not to twist cast-on row; pm for beginning of rnd.

Work around in k1, p1 ribbing for 1¼ in (3 cm). Change to larger-size circular and knit 1 rnd, increasing 2 (8) sts evenly spaced around = 90 (100) sts. Now work following chart.

When cap measures 6¾ (7) in [17 (18) cm], begin shaping crown (change to dpn when sts no longer fit around circular). Continue pattern as you shape crown.

Decrease Rnd 1: Decrease 1 st in each knit band with k2tog joining the 3rd and 4th knit sts = 6 sts rem in each knit band. Work 3 rnds in pattern.

Decrease Rnd 2: Decrease 1 st in each knit band with k2tog joining the 2 center sts = 5 sts rem in each knit band. Work 3 rnds in pattern.

Decrease Rnd 3: Decrease 1 st in each purl band with p2tog joining the 1st 2 purl sts = 2 sts rem in each purl band. Work 3 rnds in pattern.

Decrease Rnd 4: Decrease 1 st in each knit band with k2tog joining the 2nd and 3rd knit sts = 4 sts rem in each knit band. Work 1 rnd in pattern.

Decrease Rnd 5: Decrease 1 st in each knit band with k2tog joining the 2 center sts = 3 sts rem in each knit band. Work 1 rnd in pattern.

Decrease Rnd 6: Decrease 1 st in each purl band with p2tog = 1 st rem in each purl band. Work 1 rnd in pattern.

Decrease Rnd 7: Decrease 1 st in each knit band with k2tog joining the 1st 2 sts = 2 sts rem in each knit band.

Last 2 decrease rnds: K2tog around.

FINISHING

Cut yarn and draw end through rem sts; tighten. Weave in all ends neatly on WS. Sew on 2 buttons or a leather patch. Lay a damp towel over cap and leave until dry or gently steam-press cap under a damp pressing cloth.

Adult

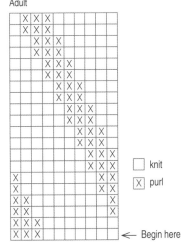

☐ knit
☒ purl

← Begin here

Parties and Holidays

Party Outfit Cardigan for Adults

An unbelievably fine cardigan to knit with an impressive two-color pattern. It is a bit time-consuming, perhaps, but your success will be obvious as the pattern emerges.

SIZES: XS–S (M, L, XL)

FINISHED MEASUREMENTS
Chest: Approx. 36 (38¾, 43¼, 46) in [91 (98.5, 110, 117) cm]
Total Length: Approx. 25½ (26, 26¾, 27¼) in [65 (66, 68, 69) cm]

MATERIALS
YARN: Sandnes Garn KlompeLompe Tynn Merinoull (fine Merino wool) [CYCA #1 – fingering, 100% Merino wool, 191 yd (175 m) / 50 g]
YARN COLORS AND AMOUNTS:
Color A 7251 (MC): 300 (350, 350, 400) g
Color B 1013: 200 (250, 250, 250) g
NEEDLES: US sizes 1.5 and 2.5 (2.5 and 3 mm): 16 and 24 in (40 and 60 cm) circulars and sets of 5 dpn or use 32 in (80 cm) circular for magic loop (see video on magic loop technique on klompelompe.no).
NOTIONS: 8 (8, 9, 9) buttons

GAUGE: 27 sts on larger-size needles = 4 in (10 cm).
Adjust needle size to obtain correct gauge if necessary.

> **Knitting Tip**
> Note that on some rounds, the yarn floats are rather long. If longer than 5 sts, twist the strands around each other on back of work for a more even result. However, do not stack twists or the colors will show through on RS.

The cardigan is worked from the top down, back and forth on a circular needle until adding a steek to knit in the round.

With smaller-size circular and color A, CO 139 (153, 161, 165) sts, Work back and forth in k1, p1 ribbing for 1⅜ in (3.5 cm).

Change to larger-size circular and knit 1 row, CO 7 sts at end of row for a steek. Steek sts are not included on the chart or in any stitch counts. Begin knitting in the round.

Knit 1 rnd, increasing 14 (16, 16, 20) sts evenly spaced around = 153 (169,177, 185) sts.

> **Knitting Tip**
> Work steek alternating colors A and B. The stripes will make it easier to cut steek open when finishing.

Begin pattern following chart A. After completing charted rows, you should have 305 (337, 353, 369) sts.

Knit 1 rnd increasing 16 (14, 28, 32) sts evenly spaced around = 321 (351, 381, 401) sts.
    Work following chart E.
    Knit 1 rnd, increasing 16 (18, 20, 16) sts evenly spaced around = 337 (369, 401, 417) sts.
    Work following chart C. Knit 1 rnd, increasing 32 (24, 16, 16) sts evenly spaced around = 369 (393, 417, 433) sts.
    Work following chart B. Knit 1 rnd, increasing 18 (14, 24, 40) sts evenly spaced around = 387 (407, 441, 473) sts.

Sizes L and XL: Work following chart D.
    Knit 0 (0, 1, 1) rnd, increasing 0 (0, 6, 4) sts evenly spaced around.

Place sts for sleeves on holders as follows (knit with MC):
    K54 (59, 67, 72), place next 85 (85, 90, 95) sts on holder, CO 12 sts for underarm, k109 (119, 133, 143) for back, place next 85 (85, 90, 95) sts on holder, CO 12 sts for underarm, k54 (59, 67, 72) = 241 (261, 291, 311) sts rem on needle.

FRONT AND BACK

Work following chart E until body measures 22½ (22¾, 23¾, 24) in [57 (58, 60, 61) cm].

Knit 1 rnd with MC and, *at the same time*, BO steek sts.

Change to smaller-size circular and work in k1, p1 ribbing for 3¼ in (8 cm). BO in ribbing on last rnd.

SLEEVES

With larger-size dpn, CO 6 sts, k85 (85, 90, 95) sts from holder, CO 6 sts.

The sleeves are knitted in the round on dpn. Always purl the 1st (marked) st with MC.

Work following chart E. When sleeve measures 1¼ in (3 cm), begin shaping as follows:

Knit until 2 sts before marked st, sl 1, k1, psso, p1, k2tog.

Note that the pattern gradually loses sts.

Decrease the same way every ¾ in (2 cm)

until 55 (59, 60, 61) sts rem.

Continue in pattern until sleeve is 15¾ in (40 cm) long or desired length. Knit 1 rnd with MC, decreasing 1 (1, 0, 1) st.

Change to smaller-size dpn and work in k1, p1 ribbing for 3¼ in (8 cm). BO in ribbing. Make 2nd sleeve the same way.

FINISHING

Machine-stitch 2 fine lines on each side of the center steek stitch. Carefully cut steek open up center stitch. With smaller-size circular and MC, pick up and knit 3 sts for every 4 rows along left front edge. Pick up an odd number of sts and work 8 rows in k1, p1 ribbing. BO in ribbing (make sure bind-off is not too tight).

Make buttonhole band on right front as for left band. But, on row 3, make 8 (8, 9, 9) buttonholes evenly spaced down band: for each buttonhole, BO 2 sts and CO 2 sts over

each gap on next row.

Fold cut steek edge to WS and tack down smoothly with fine stitches. If it is difficult to make a smooth fold, you can knit a facing to sew over the steek. On WS, with MC, pick up and knit sts as for button bands and work back and forth in stockinette until facing covers steek. BO and sew down facing to WS using MC so stitching won't show.

Seam underarms and sew on buttons. Weave in all ends neatly on WS.

Lay a damp towel over sweater and leave until dry or gently steam-press sweater under a damp pressing cloth.

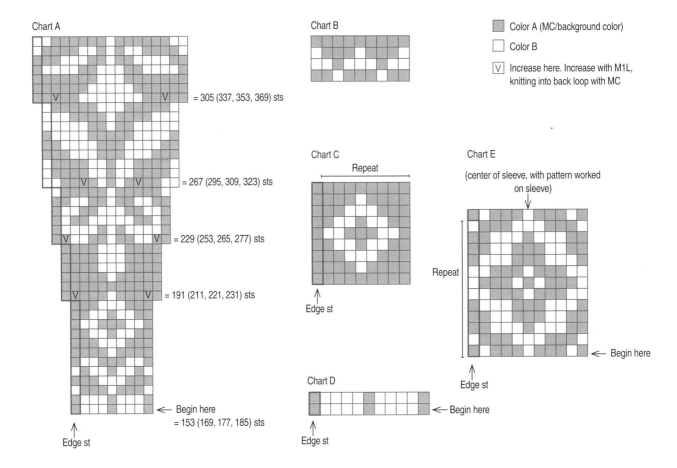

Party Outfit Stocking Cap

Complete your party outfit with an impressive cap.

SIZES: 0–2 (2–4, 4–9, 12, 18–24 months, 3–4, 5–6 years)

MATERIALS

YARN: Sandnes Garn KlompeLompe Tynn Merinoull (fine Merino wool) [CYCA #1 – fingering, 100% Merino wool, 191 yd (175 m) / 50 g]

YARN COLORS AND AMOUNTS:

Color A 7251 (MC): 50 (50, 50, 50, 50, 50, 50) g
Color B 1013: 50 (50, 50, 50, 50, 50, 50) g

NEEDLES: US sizes 1.5 and 2.5 (2.5 and 3 mm): 16 in (40 cm) circulars and set of 5 dpn or use 32 in (80 cm) circular for magic loop (see video on magic loop technique on klompelompe.no).

GAUGE: 27 sts on larger-size needles = 4 in (10 cm).
Adjust needle size to obtain correct gauge if necessary.

With smaller-size circular and color A, CO 80 (88, 92, 104, 112, 120) sts, Join, being careful not to twist cast-on row; pm for beginning of rnd. Work around in k1, p1 ribbing for 10 (10, 12, 12, 14, 14, 14) rnds

Change to larger-size circular and knit 1 rnd increasing 0 (2, 8, 4, 6, 8, 0) sts evenly spaced around = 80 (90,100, 100, 110, 120, 120) sts

Now work around following chart until cap measures 3½ (4, 4, 4¼, 4¾, 5¼, 5½) in [9 (10, 10, 11, 12, 13, 14) cm].
Pm on each side as follows: beginning of rnd marker, k40 (45, 50, 50, 55, 60, 60) in pattern, pm, k40 (45, 50, 50, 55, 60, 60) in pattern.

Continue in pattern in each section while you decrease at the sides:
Decrease Rnd 1: Knit to side marker, k2tog, knit to next side marker, k2tog.
Knit 1 rnd without decreasing.
Decrease Rnd 2: Knit until 2 sts before side marker, sl 1, k1, psso, knit until 2 sts before next side marker, sl 1, k1, psso.
Knit 1 rnd without decreasing.

Rep these 4 rows until 8 sts rem.

FINISHING

Cut yarn. Draw end through rem 8 sts and tighten.
Weave in all ends neatly on WS.
Lay a damp towel over cap and leave until dry or gently steam-press cap under a damp pressing cloth.

■ Color A (MC/background color)
□ Color B

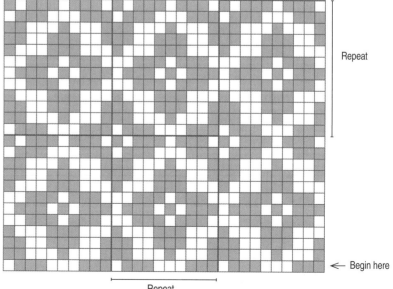

Repeat

← Begin here

Repeat

Party Outfit Cardigan for Children

Our version of a traditional knit. The cardigan has an all-over two-color stranded knit pattern for an interesting knitting project. The sweater will be just right for celebrating any big occasion.

Level 3

SIZES: 1 (2, 4, 6, 8, 10, 12) years

FINISHED MEASUREMENTS
Chest: Approx. 22¾ (24¼, 25½, 27¼, 30, 31½, 33) in [58 (61.5, 65, 69, 76, 80, 84) cm]
Total Length: Approx. 13 (15, 16½, 18¼, 19½, 20½, 22) in [33 (38, 42, 46.5, 49.5, 52, 56) cm]

MATERIALS
YARN: Sandnes Garn KlompeLompe Tynn Merinoull (fine Merino wool) [CYCA #1 – fingering, 100% Merino wool, 191 yd (175 m) / 50 g]
YARN COLORS AND AMOUNTS:
Color A 1042 (MC): 150 (150, 150, 200, 250, 250, 300) g
Color B 1015: 100 (100, 100, 100, 150, 150, 200) g
NEEDLES: US sizes 1.5 and 2.5 (2.5 and 3 mm): 16 and 24 in (40 and 60 cm) circulars and sets of 5 dpn or use 32 in (80 cm) circular for magic loop (see video on magic loop technique on klompelompe.no).
NOTIONS: 7 (8, 8, 8, 9, 9, 9) buttons

GAUGE: 27 sts on larger-size needles = 4 in (10 cm).
Adjust needle size to obtain correct gauge if necessary.

On Henry: Party Outfit Cardigan: color A 1042, color B 1013
Party Outfit Pants: color A 1055, color B 1013
Party Outfit Socks: color 1013
On Tilda: Party Outfit Cardigan: color A 4331, color B 1013
Party Outfit Skirt: color A 4331, color B1013

(265, 279, 303, 313, 331, 341) sts, spacing increases evenly around.

Sizes 4, 8, 10, and 12: Work following chart C.

Sizes 2, 6, 10, and 12: Work following chart B.

Place sts for sleeves on holders as follows (knit with MC):

K34 (37, 38, 44, 45, 48, 50), place next 55 (59, 61, 63, 63, 67, 67) sts on holder, CO 7 sts for underarm, k69 (73, 81, 89, 97, 101, 107) for back, place next 55 (59, 61, 63, 63, 67, 67) sts on holder, CO 7 sts for underarm, k34 (37, 38, 44, 45, 48, 50 = 151 (161, 171, 191, 201, 211, 221) sts rem on needle.

FRONT AND BACK

Work following chart D. Knit 2 rnds with MC and then work following chart until body measures 11¾ (13¾, 15½, 17, 18¼, 19, 20½) in [30 (35, 39, 43, 46, 48, 52) cm].

Knit 1 rnd with MC (color A) and, *at the same time*, BO steek sts.

Change to smaller-size circular and work in k1, p1 ribbing for 1¼ (1¼, 1¼, 1⅜, 1⅜, 1½, 1½) in [3 (3, 3, 3.5, 3.5, 4, 4 cm)]. BO in ribbing.

SLEEVES

With larger-size dpn, CO 4 sts, k55 (59, 61, 63, 63, 67, 67) sts from holder, CO 3 sts.

The sleeves are knitted in the round on dpn. Always purl the 1st (marked) st with MC.

Work following chart D. Knit 2 rnds with MC and then work following chart E. When sleeve measures 1¼ in (3 cm), begin shaping as follows:

Knit until 2 sts before marked st, sl 1, k1, psso, p1, k2tog.

Note that the pattern gradually loses sts.

Decrease the same way every 1¼ in (3 cm) until 50 (52, 54, 54, 56, 58, 62) sts rem.

Continue in pattern until sleeve is 7 (8¼, 9½, 10¾, 11¾, 13, 14½) in [18 (21, 24, 27, 30, 33, 37 cm) long or desired length. Knit 1 rnd with MC, decreasing 6 (4, 6, 4, 6, 2, 6) sts evenly spaced around.

Back: color A 6061, color B 1020. Front: color A 4331, color B 1013.

The cardigan is worked from the top down, back and forth on a circular needle until adding a steek to knit in the round.

With smaller-size circular and color A, CO 89 (93, 99, 99, 107, 107, 113) sts, Work back and forth in k1, p1 ribbing for 1 (1, 1¼, 1¼, 1¼, 1⅜, 1⅜) in [2.5 (2.5, 3, 3, 3, 3.5, 3.5) cm].

Change to larger-size circular and knit 1 row, CO 7 sts at end of row for a steek. Steek sts are not included on the chart or in any stitch counts. Begin knitting in the round.

Knit 1 rnd, increasing 48 (52, 46, 54, 54, 54, 56) sts evenly spaced around = 137 (145, 145, 153, 161, 161, 169 sts.
Begin pattern following chart A. After completing charted rows, you should have 239 (253, 253, 305, 321, 321, 337) sts. Knit 1 rnd, adjusting stitch count to 247

Change to smaller-size dpn and work in k1, p1 ribbing for 1¼ (1¼, 1¼, 1⅜, 1⅜, 1½, 1½) in [3 (3, 3, 3.5, 3.5, 4, 4 cm)]. BO in ribbing.

Make 2nd sleeve the same way.

FINISHING
Machine-stitch 2 fine lines on each side of the center steek stitch. Carefully cut steek open up center stitch.
Buttonhole Band: on left side for boy's version and right side for girl's.

With smaller-size circular and MC, pick up and knit 3 sts for every 4 rows along left front edge. Pick up an odd number of sts and work 8 rows in k1, p1 ribbing. BO in ribbing (make sure bind-off is not too tight).

Make buttonhole band on as for button band. But, on row 3, make 7 (8, 8, 8, 9, 9, 9) buttonholes evenly spaced down band: for each buttonhole, BO 2 sts and CO 2 sts over each gap on next row.

Fold cut steek edge to WS and sew down smoothly with fine stitches. If it is difficult to make a smooth fold, you can knit a facing to

sew over the steek. On WS, with MC, pick up and knit sts as for button bands and work back and forth in stockinette until facing covers steek. BO and sew down facing to WS using MC so stitching won't show.

Seam underarms and sew on buttons. Weave in all ends neatly on WS.
Lay a damp towel over sweater and leave until dry or gently steam-press sweater under a damp pressing cloth.

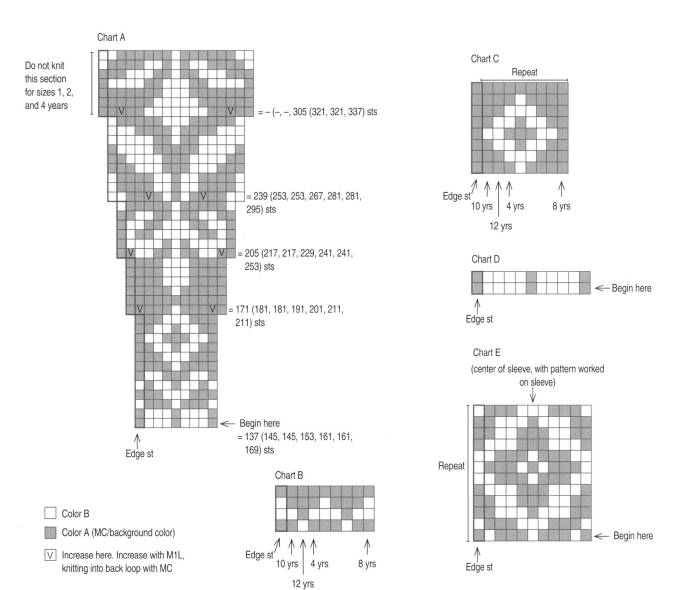

Chart A

Do not knit this section for sizes 1, 2, and 4 years

= – (–, –, –, 305 (321, 321, 337) sts

= 239 (253, 253, 267, 281, 281, 295) sts

= 205 (217, 217, 229, 241, 241, 253) sts

= 171 (181, 181, 191, 201, 211, 211) sts

← Begin here
= 137 (145, 145, 153, 161, 161, 169) sts

Edge st

☐ Color B

▨ Color A (MC/background color)

Ⅴ Increase here. Increase with M1L, knitting into back loop with MC

Chart B

Edge st
10 yrs   4 yrs   8 yrs
12 yrs

Chart C

Repeat

Edge st
10 yrs   4 yrs   8 yrs
12 yrs

Chart D

← Begin here

Edge st

Chart E
(center of sleeve, with pattern worked on sleeve)

Repeat

← Begin here

Edge st

Party Outfit Pinafore

A simple pinafore in KlompeLompe style. The belt pattern on the skirt is adapted from the Party Outfit Cardigan. Choose wood buttons for an informal outfit or pewter buttons for a fancier outfit.

SIZES: 1–3 (6–9 months, 1, 2, 4, 6, 8) years

FINISHED MEASUREMENTS
Chest: Approx. 17½ (19, 19, 20½, 20½, 21¾, 21¾) in [44.5 (48, 48, 52, 52, 55.5, 55.5) cm]
Total Length, excluding straps: Approx. 9½ (10¾, 11¾, 13, 13¾, 15½, 17¾) in [24 (27, 30, 33, 35, 39, 45) cm]

MATERIALS
YARN: Sandnes Garn KlompeLompe Tynn Merinoull (fine Merino wool) [CYCA #1 – fingering, 100% Merino wool, 191 yd (175 m) / 50 g]
YARN COLORS AND AMOUNTS:
Color A 4331 (MC): 100 (100, 100, 200, 200, 200, 200) g
Color B 1013: 50 (50, 50, 50, 50, 50, 50) g
NEEDLES: US sizes 1.5 and 2.5 (2.5 and 3 mm): 16 and 24 in (40 and 60 cm) circulars and sets of 5 dpn or use 32 in (80 cm) circular for magic loop (see video on magic loop technique on klompelompe.no).
NOTIONS: 8 buttons; optional: waistband elastic, long enough to go through waistband + seam allowance

GAUGE: 27 sts on larger-size needles = 4 in (10 cm).
Adjust needle size to obtain correct gauge if necessary.

The pinafore begins at the "belt" at the waist and is knitted in the round on a circular needle. The round begins at the front so the join is hidden under the bib.

With smaller-size circular and MC, CO 120 (130, 130, 140, 140, 150, 150) sts. Join, being careful not to twist cast-on row; pm for beginning of rnd. Work 13 rnds k1, p1 ribbing, purl 1 rnd for foldline, and then continue in charted pattern.

Knit 1 rnd in MC; cut yarn. Slip 60 (65, 65, 70, 70, 75, 75) sts to right needle.
    The rnd now begins at this point, center back.

Change to larger-size circular.
Knit 1 rnd, increasing 30 (30, 34, 34, 36, 34, 38) sts evenly spaced around = 150 (160, 164, 174, 176, 184,188) sts.
    Knit 6 rnds. Place sts on a holder while you begin bib.

BIB
Begin with back of bib. With larger-size needle and MC, pick up and knit 32 (36, 38, 42, 42, 48, 48) sts centered on front on top of belt.
    Work back and forth in stockinette for 1½ (2, 2½, 2¾, 2¾, 3¼, 3½) in [4 (5, 6, 7, 7, 8, 9) cm].
    Make buttonholes as follows:
    K3, BO 2 sts, knit until 5 sts rem, BO 2 sts, k3.

On next row (WS), CO 2 sts over each gap.
    Work 3 rows in stockinette.
    On next row (WS), knit all sts = foldline. Now begin the front of the bib.
    Work 3 rows in stockinette.

    Make buttonholes as before but on WS, as follows:
    P3, BO 2 sts, purl until 5 sts rem, BO 2 sts, p3.
On next row (RS), CO 2 sts over each gap.

Work in stockinette until same length as to place where you changed to larger-size needle on "belt."
    Now increase on each side on every RS row follows: K1, M1, knit until 1 st rem, M1, k1.
    After increasing 3 times at each side = 38 (42, 44, 48, 48, 54, 54) sts and next row is on RS, cut yarn and begin at back of skirt, where you ended before you began the bib.

K56 (59, 60, 63, 64, 65, 67), join skirt and bib by knitting together: 1 st from bib with 1 st of skirt across, ending with k56 (59, 60, 63, 64, 65, 67).
    Knit 1 rnd, increasing 0 (0, 1, 1, 4, 1, 2) sts evenly spaced around = 150 (160, 165, 175, 180, 185, 190) sts.
    Knit 1 rnd and place 5 markers with 30 (32, 33, 35, 36, 37, 38) sts between each marker.

On next rnd, increase at markers as follows: *Knit until 2 sts before marker, M1, knit until 2 sts after marker, M1*; rep * to * around = 10 sts increased around = 160 (170, 175, 185, 190, 195, 200) sts.

Rep the increases every 1¼ in (3 cm) until there are 190 (200, 225, 235, 240, 255, 260) sts. Continue in stockinette until skirt measures 7½ (8¼, 9, 9¾, 10¾, 11¾, 13¾) in [19 (21, 23, 25, 27, 30, 35) cm] below belt.

Purl 1 rnd (foldline) and then knit 6 rnds. BO.

FINISHING

Sew back of belt to front of belt. If desired, insert elastic through waistband before you seam it totally.

Seam sides of bib and sew a couple of sts on each side of buttonholes to keep back and front of bib together.

Weave in all ends neatly on WS.

STRAPS

With MC and smaller-size needles, pick up and knit 19 (19, 21, 23, 23, 25, 25) sts at center back. Work 10 rows in k1, p1 ribbing. On next row, BO the center st and work each strap separately. Continue in ribbing until strap measures 8¾ (9¾, 11¾, 13¾, 15, 15¾, 15¾) in [22 (25, 30, 35, 38, 40, 40) cm] from picked-up sts.

Sew 2 buttons to each strap so you can adjust the size.

Sew 2 buttons on each side of the bib at the belt and directly below it for decoration.

Lay a damp towel over pinafore and leave until dry or gently steam-press pinafore under a damp pressing cloth.

☐ Color A (MC)
☐ Color B

← Begin here

Repeat

Party Outfit Socks

Party Outfit Socks, for both boys and girls,
to wear with the beautiful ensemble.

SIZES: 1–3 (6–9 months, 1, 2, 4, 6 years)

MATERIALS

YARN: Sandnes Garn KlompeLompe Tynn Merinoull (fine Merino wool) [CYCA #1 – fingering, 100% Merino wool, 191 yd (175 m) / 50 g]

YARN COLORS AND AMOUNTS:
Color 1013: 50 (50, 50, 50, 100, 100) g

NEEDLES: US size 2.5 (3 mm): set of 5 dpn or 32 in (80 cm) circular for magic loop (see video on magic loop technique on klompelompe.no).

GAUGE: 27 sts on larger size needles = 4 in (10 cm).
Adjust needle size to obtain correct gauge if necessary.

CO 36 (40, 46, 46, 52, 52) sts on dpn or magic loop circular; join.
Work around in k2, p2 ribbing for ¾ in (2 cm).
Next rnd: Knit, increasing 6 (8, 8, 8, 8, 8) sts evenly spaced around = 42 (48, 54, 54, 60, 60) sts.
Next rnd (= Rnd 1 of pattern): Work 3 (5, 6, 6, 8, 8) sts in k1, p1 ribbing, pm, 14 sts in pattern, pm, 7 (10, 13, 13, 16, 16) sts in k1, p1 ribbing, pm, 14 sts pattern, pm, 4 (5, 7, 7, 8, 8) sts k1, p1 ribbing.
Continue in pattern over pattern sts and ribbing over ribbing.
Work pattern repeat a total of 3 (4, 6, 6, 7, 8) times.

PATTERN REPEAT
(A MULTIPLE OF 14 STS)
Rnd 1: Knit.
Rnd 2: Knit.
Rnd 3: K5, k2tog, yo, sl 1, k1, psso, k5 = 13 sts rem.
Rnd 4: Knit.
Rnd 5: K4, k2tog, yo, k1, yo, sl 1, k1, psso, k4.
Rnd 6: Knit.
Rnd 7: K3, k2tog, yo, k3, yo, sl 1, k1, psso, k3.
Rnd 8: Knit.
Rnd 9: K4, yo, k1, sl 1, k2, psso, k1, yo, k4 = 14 sts.
Rnd 10: Knit

HEEL
Now work the heel over the 1st 21 (24, 27, 27, 30, 30) sts.
Knit until 1 st rem; turn, sl 1 and purl until 1 st rem.
Turn, sl 1, knit until 2 sts rem.
Turn, sl 1, purl until 2 sts rem.
Continue turning the same way with 1 st less on each row until 7 (8, 9, 9, 10, 10) sts rem.
There will be 3 sections—side-middle-side with the same number of sts in each.
Now begin increasing back to 21 (24, 27, 27, 30, 30) sts:
Work until 1 st before gap. Sl 1, M1 and k/p it tog with st on left needle. Turn and sl 1. Work until 1 st before gap. Sl 1, M1 and k/p it tog with st on left needle. Turn and sl 1. Continue the same way until all the sts have been worked and 21 (24, 27, 27, 30, 30) sts rem.

Now work over all the sts, M1 and knit it tog with the next st on each side of the heel to avoid a hole.

Knit 1 rnd, decreasing 6 (8, 8, 8, 8, 8) sts evenly spaced around = 36 (40, 46, 46, 52, 52) sts. Work in pattern on the instep and in stockinette on the sole until foot measures 3¼ (3½, 3½, 4¼, 5¼, 5 ½) in [8 (9, 9, 11, 13, 14) cm].

Pm on each side (beginning of rnd and after 18 (20, 23, 23, 26, 26) sts).
Shape toe as follows: K1, k2tog, knit until 3 sts before marker, k2tog, k2, k2tog, knit until 3 sts before marker, k2tog, k1.
Decrease the same way on every other rnd a total of 2 (3, 3, 3, 5, 5) times. Then, decrease on every rnd a total of 4 (4, 5, 5, 5, 5) times = 12 (12, 14, 14, 12, 12) sts rem.

Cut yarn and draw end through rem sts; tighten. Weave in all ends neatly on WS.

Party Outfit Rompers

Simple rompers with adjustable straps and the pretty Party Outfit pattern on the belt.

SIZES: 1–3 (6–9 months, 1, 2, 4, 6 years)

FINISHED MEASUREMENTS
Chest (measured without the waist band): Approx. 17½ (19, 19, 20½, 20½, 21¾) in [44.5 (48, 48, 52, 52, 55.5) cm]
Total Length, excluding straps: Approx. 12¾ (15½, 18¼, 21, 24¾, 27½) in [32 (39, 46, 53, 63, 70) cm]

MATERIALS
YARN: Sandnes Garn KlompeLompe Tynn Merinoull (fine Merino wool) [CYCA #1 – fingering, 100% Merino wool, 191 yd (175 m) / 50 g]
YARN COLORS AND AMOUNTS:
Color A 6061 (MC): 100 (150, 150, 200, 200, 200) g
Color B 1013: 50 (50, 50, 50, 50, 50) g
NEEDLES: US sizes 1.5 and 2.5 (2.5 and 3 mm): 16 and 24 in (40 and 60 cm) circulars and sets of 5 dpn or use 32 in (80 cm) circular for magic loop (see video on magic loop technique on klompelompe.no).
NOTIONS: 10 decorative buttons; optional: waistband elastic, long enough to go around each leg and through waistband + seam allowances.

GAUGE: 27 sts on larger-size needles = 4 in (10 cm).
Adjust needle size to obtain correct gauge if necessary.

The rompers, knitted in the round on a circular needle, begin at the "belt" on the waist. The round begins at the front so the join is hidden under the bib.

With smaller-size circular and MC, CO 120 (130, 130, 140, 140, 150) sts. Join, being careful not to twist cast-on row; pm for beginning of rnd. Work 13 rnds k1, p1 ribbing, purl 1 rnd for foldline and then continue in charted pattern.

Knit 1 rnd in MC; cut yarn. Slip 60 (65, 65, 70, 70, 75) sts to right needle.
The rnd now begins at this point, center back.

Change to larger-size circular.
Knit 1 rnd, increasing 14 (12, 16, 10, 14, 16) sts evenly spaced around = 134 (142, 146, 150, 154, 166) sts.
Make the pants higher on the back with short rows (when you come to a yarnover, knit/purl it together with the next st):
K10; turn, yo, p20; turn, yo, k25; turn, yo, p30; turn, yo, k35; turn yo, p40; turn, yo, k45; turn, yo, p50; turn, yo, knit to beginning of rnd.
Knit 6 rnds. Slip sts to a holder while you begin knitting the bib.

BIB
Begin with back of bib. With larger size needle and MC, pick up and knit 32 (36, 38, 42, 42, 48) sts centered on front on top of belt.

Work back and forth in stockinette for 1½ (2, 2½, 2¾, 2¾, 3¼) in [4 (5, 6, 7, 7, 8) cm].
Make buttonholes as follows:
K3, BO 2 sts, knit until 5 sts rem, BO 2 sts, k3.
On next row (WS), CO 2 sts over each gap.
Work 3 rows in stockinette.
On next row (WS), knit all sts = foldline. Now begin the front of the bib.
Work 3 rows in stockinette.
Make buttonholes as before but on WS, as follows:
P3, BO 2 sts, purl until 5 sts rem, BO 2 sts, p3.
On next row (RS), CO 2 sts over each gap.

Work in stockinette until same length as to place where you changed to larger-size needle on "belt."
Now increase on each side every time you are on RS as follows: K1, M1, knit until 1 st rem, M1, k1.
After increasing 3 times at each side = 38 (42, 44, 48, 48, 54) sts and next row is on RS, cut yarn and begin at back of rompers, where you ended before you began the bib.

K48 (50, 51, 51, 53, 56); join pants and bib by knitting together 1 st from bib with 1 st of pants across, ending with k48 (50, 51, 51, 53, 56).
Continue in stockinette until whole piece measures 8¼ (10¼, 12¼, 14¼, 15¾, 17¼) in [21 (26, 31, 36, 40, 44) cm] from top edge of bib.

Pm at each side of the 8 center front and back sts.

Increase 1 st with M1 on each side of the 8 sts = 4 sts increased. Increase the same way on every 3rd rnd a total of 5 times = 20 new sts. Knit 1 rnd and then BO the center 8 sts at back and front.

Work each leg separately, on dpn or magic loop circular = 69 (73, 75, 77, 79, 85) sts.

Note: The decreases under the leg occur more widely spread out on sizes 1-4 years but not on the 2 smallest sizes.

Pm at beginning of rnd (or purl 1st st on every rnd). Knit around for ¾ in (2 cm). Begin shaping as follows: K1, k2tog, knit until 3 sts rem, sl 1, k1, psso, k1.

Decrease the same way every ¾ in (2 cm) a total of 0 (0, 3, 4, 4, 5) times = 69 (73, 69, 69, 71, 75) sts rem.

Continue in stockinette until leg measures 2½ (3¼, 4, 4¾, 7, 8¼) in [6 (8, 10, 12, 18, 21) cm].

Knit 1 rnd, decreasing 25 (27, 21, 19, 21, 25) sts evenly spaced around = 44 (46, 48, 50, 50, 50) sts rem.

Change to smaller-size dpn/magic loop. Knit 8 rnds. BO on last rnd. Work 2nd leg the same way.

FINISHING

Fold facings in on foldline and sew down on WS. If desired, sew elastic in lower edge of each pants leg.

Sew back of belt to front of belt. If desired, insert elastic into waistband before you seam it totally.

Seam sides of bib and sew a couple of sts on each side of buttonholes to keep back and front of bib together.

Seam bib with Kitchener st. Weave in all ends neatly on WS.

STRAPS

With MC and smaller size needles, pick up and knit 19 (19, 21, 23, 23, 25) sts at center back. Work 10 rows in k1, p1 ribbing. On next row, BO the center st and work each strap separately. Continue in ribbing until strap measures 8¾ (9¾, 11¾, 13¾, 15, 15¾) in [22 (25, 30, 35, 38, 40) cm] from picked-up sts. BO in ribbing.

Sew 2 buttons to each strap so you can adjust the size.

Sew 2 buttons on each side of the bib at the belt and directly below it for decoration. Sew an extra button on outer side of lower edge of each leg.

Lay a damp towel over rompers and leave until dry or gently steam-press rompers under a damp pressing cloth.

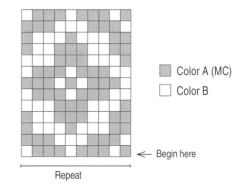

Color A (MC)

Color B

← Begin here

Repeat

Party Outfit Cardigan for Baby

Of course, baby must have a party outfit cardigan. This one is knitted with raglan shaping and only one of the patterns from the Party Outfit Cardigan.

SIZES: 0–1 (3, 6, 9–12) months

FINISHED MEASUREMENTS
Chest: Approx. 17¾ (19, 20½, 22) in [45 (48.5, 52, 56) cm]
Total Length: Approx. 10¼ (11, 12¾, 13½) in [26 (28, 32, 34) cm]

MATERIALS
YARN: Sandnes Garn KlompeLompe Tynn Merinoull (fine Merino wool) [CYCA #1 – fingering, 100% Merino wool, 191 yd (175 m) / 50 g]

YARN COLORS AND AMOUNTS:
Color A 4344 (MC): 100 (100, 100, 100) g
Color B 1013: 50 (50, 50, 100) g
NEEDLES: US sizes 1.5 and 2.5 (2.5 and 3 mm): 16 in (40 cm) circulars and sets of 5 dpn or use 32 in (80 cm) circular for magic loop (see video on magic loop technique on klompelompe.no).
NOTIONS: 5 (5, 6, 6) buttons

GAUGE: 27 sts on larger size needles = 4 in (10 cm).
Adjust needle size to obtain correct gauge if necessary.

The cardigan is worked from the top down, back and forth on a circular needle until adding a steek to knit in the round.

With smaller-size circular and color A, CO 121 (131, 141, 151) sts, Work10 rows back and forth in k1, p1 ribbing.

Change to larger-size circular and CO 6 sts at beginning of row for a steek. Steek sts are not included on the chart or in any stitch counts.
Begin knitting in the round.

Work in pattern following chart until body measures 5½ (6¼, 7, 8) in [14 (16, 18, 20) cm].
Next rnd: Work 27 (29, 32, 34) sts in pattern, BO 7 sts, work 53 (59, 63, 69) sts in pattern, BO 7 sts, work 27 (29, 32, 34) sts in pattern.
  Set body aside while you knit sleeves.

SLEEVES
With smaller-size dpn and color A, CO 38 (38, 42, 42) sts, Divide sts onto dpn and join. Work 10 rnds in k1, p1 ribbing.
  Change to larger-size dpn. Knit 1 rnd, increasing 4 (4, 10, 10) sts evenly spaced around = 42 (42, 52, 52) sts.
  The 1st on the needle is a marked st and always purled with color A all the way up sleeve.
  Work following chart.
  When sleeve is 2½ in (6 cm) long, increase with M1, 1 st before and 1 st after marked st.

Work new sts at beginning and end of rnd into pattern.
  Increase the same way every ⅜ (⅝, ¾, ¾) in [1 (1.5, 2, 2) cm] until there are 54 (56, 64, 66) sts. Then continue in pattern until sleeve is 5¼ (6 , 7, 8) in [13 (16, 18, 20) cm] long.
  Next rnd: BO 4 sts, wok in pattern until 3 sts rem, BO 3 sts.
Set 1st sleeve aside while you knit 2nd sleeve the same way.

Place sleeves on same circular with body, matching underarms, and begin yoke. At the intersection of each piece, CO 1 st (marked st), which is always purled with color A. Work 2 rnds.

  Continue in pattern following chart on each piece.
  On the next rnd, begin yoke shaping as follows:
  Work in pattern until 2 sts before marked st, sl 1, k1, psso, purl marked st, k2tog. Rep the decreases at each marked st = 8 sts decreased around.
  When decreasing, use the color that fits best into pattern. Decrease on every other rnd a total of 15 (18, 20, 22) times.
  Knit 1 rnd with color A and then BO steek sts.
  Change to smaller-size circular and work 8 rows in k1, p1 ribbing.
  BO in ribbing on last row.

FINISHING

Machine-stitch 2 fine lines on each side of the center steek stitch. Carefully cut steek open up center stitch.

Buttonhole Band: on left side for boy's version and right side for girl's.

With smaller-size circular and color A, pick up and knit 3 sts for every 4 rows along left front edge. Pick up an odd number of sts and work 8 rows in k1, p1 ribbing. BO in ribbing (make sure bind-off is not too tight). Make buttonhole band as for button band. But, on row 3, make 5 (5, 6, 6) buttonholes evenly spaced down band: for each buttonhole, BO 2 sts and CO 2 sts over each gap on next (4th) row.

Fold cut steek edge to WS and sew down smoothly with fine stitches. If it is difficult to make a smooth fold, you can knit a facing to sew over the steek. On WS, with MC, pick up and knit sts as for button bands and work back and forth in stockinette until facing covers steek. BO and sew down facing to WS using MC so stitching won't show.

Seam underarms and sew on buttons. Weave in all ends neatly on WS.

Lay a damp towel over sweater and leave until dry or gently steam-press sweater under a damp pressing cloth.

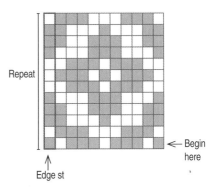

Repeat

← Begin here

↑ Edge st

84

Alise Fine Cardigan
for Women

A cropped sweater for special occasions, it is especially pretty over a dress. It is so delicate that it could be worn for a wedding, and the elegant yarn comes in several light shades suitable for a bridal dress.
We like it just as well with jeans.

SIZES: XS (S, M, L, XL)

FINISHED MEASUREMENTS
Chest: Approx. 31½ (34, 36¼, 38½, 41) in [80 (86, 92, 98, 104) cm]
Total Length: Approx. 15½ (15¾, 16¼, 17, 17¾) in [39 (40, 41, 43, 45) cm]

MATERIALS
YARN: Sandnes Garn Alpakka Silke [CYCA #1 – fingering, 70% alpaca, 30% silk, 20% nylon, 219 yd (200 m) / 50 g]
YARN COLORS AND AMOUNTS:
Color 1042: 200 (200, 200, 250, 250) g
NEEDLES: US sizes 1.5 and 2.5 (2.5 and 3 mm): circulars and sets of 5 dpn
NOTIONS: 2 buttons

CROCHET HOOK: US size C-2 (2.5 mm)

GAUGE: 27 sts on larger-size needles = 4 in (10 cm).
Adjust needle size to obtain correct gauge if necessary.

The sweater begins at the lower edge and is worked back and forth on a circular needle.

BODY
With smaller-size circular, CO 217 (233, 249, 265, 281) sts.

Work back and forth in seed st for 1 in (2.5 cm):
Row 1: (K1, p1) across, end with k1.
Subsequent Rows: Work purl over knit and knit over purl.
At the same time: On 1st row, pm:
Work 76 (84, 92, 100, 108) seed sts, pm, work 65 seed sts, pm, work 76 (84, 92, 100, 108) seed sts.

Change to larger-size circular. The 5 outermost sts at each side are edge sts and are worked in seed st throughout. The rest of the body is worked in stockinette but with the pattern following the chart between the 2 markers.

Continue in stockinette with pattern between the markers until body measures 9 (9, 9, 9½, 9½) in [23 (23, 23, 24, 24) cm].
On the last row, RS, BO 10 sts at each side for the armholes as follows:
Work 5 seed sts, k44 (48, 52, 56, 60), BO 10 sts, k17 (21, 25, 29, 33), work 65 sts in charted pattern, k17 (21, 25, 29, 33), BO 10 sts, k44 (48, 52, 56, 60), work 5 seed sts.

Set body aside while you knit sleeves.

SLEEVES
With smaller-size dpn, CO 62 (66, 70, 74, 78) sts. Divide sts onto dpn and join.
Work around in seed st for 1 in (2.5 cm).

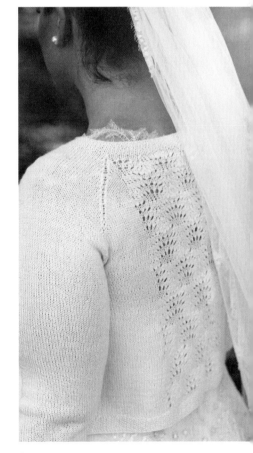

Color 1002

Change to larger-size needles. Always purl the 1st (marked) st for center of underarm.

The sleeve is worked in stockinette. When sleeve measures 1¼ in (3 cm), increase 1 st with M1 on each side of marked st (the purl st). Increase the same way every 2 in (2.5 cm) until there are 76 (80, 86, 92, 98) sts.

BO marked st. Continue in the round until sleeve measures 11¾ in (30 cm) or desired length.

Next rnd: BO 10 sts centered on underarm. Set sleeve aside while you knit 2nd sleeve the same way.

Place sleeves on circular with body, matching underarms = 327 (351, 379, 407, 435) sts total.

Pm for raglan lines at each intersection of body and sleeve = 4 markers.

Continue in stockinette, with pattern between markers and seed st on the 5 outermost sts at each side.

The 1st row = WS.

Shape raglan, decreasing at each raglan marker as follows:

Work as est until 2 sts before next marker, sl 1, k1, psso, k2tog; rep * to * , across, ending with front as est to end of row = 8 sts decreased.

Note: If the decreases occur within the pattern, work affected pattern sts in stockinette.

Continue as est until you've decreased a total of 21 (23, 26, 28, 31) times.

Purl 1 row on WS. Knit 1 row, decreasing 6 (14, 16, 26, 26) sts evenly spaced across.

NECKBAND
Change to smaller-size circular, Work 1 in (2.5 cm) in seed st and then BO in seed st.

With crochet hook, make 2 button loops at top of neck band on left side.

Attach yarn with 1 sl st in corner and ch 4. Attach chain with 1 sl st about ⅝ in (1.5 cm) lower on edge (so loop lies evenly between

the edge sts). Work 4 sl sts along edge and then make another button loop. Finish with 1 sl st.

Abbreviations:
sl st = slip stitch
ch = chain stitch

FINISHING
Weave in all ends neatly on WS. Sew on 2 buttons.
Lay a damp towel over sweater and leave until dry or gently steam-press sweater under a damp pressing cloth.

Work part A 1st and then part B. Rep these 2 charts.

Part A

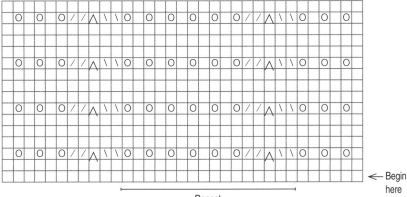

Repeat

← Begin here

Part B

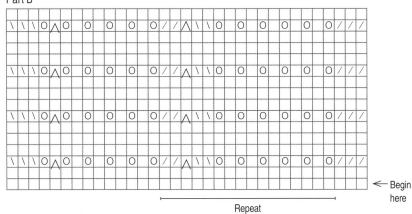

Repeat

← Begin here

☐ knit on RS, purl on WS

Ｏ yo

╱ k2tog

╲ sl 1, k1, psso (or ssk)

Λ CDD: sl 2 sts as if to knit together, k1, psso
    = 2 sts decreased

On Tilda (left): color 6041, on Tora: color 6052 ⟶

Alise Fine Cardigan for Children

A cropped sweater that is especially lovely worn over a dress. It sparks up an outfit with its fine pattern on the back and the light silk/alpaca yarn.

SIZES: 1 (2, 4, 6, 8, 10, 12) years

FINISHED MEASUREMENTS

Chest: Approx. 31¾ (22¾, 24½, 25¼, 26½, 27½, 28) in [55 (58, 62.5, 64, 67, 70, 71.5) cm]

Total Length: Approx. 9 (10¼, 11, 11½, 11¾, 13½, 14¼) in [23 (26, 28, 29, 30, 34, 36) cm]

MATERIALS

YARN: Sandnes Garn Alpakka Silke [CYCA #1 – fingering, 70% alpaca, 30% silk, 20% nylon, 219 yd (200 m) / 50 g]

YARN COLORS AND AMOUNTS:

Color 6041: 100 (100, 100, 100, 150, 150, 150) g

NEEDLES: US sizes 1.5 and 2.5 (2.5 and 3 mm): circulars and sets of 5 dpn

CROCHET HOOK: US size C-2 (2.5 mm)

NOTIONS: 2 buttons

GAUGE: 27 sts on larger-size needles = 4 in (10 cm).

Adjust needle size to obtain correct gauge if necessary.

The sweater begins at the lower edge and is worked back and forth on a circular needle.

BODY

With smaller-size circular, CO 149 (157, 169, 173, 171, 189, 193) sts.

Work back and forth in seed st for ¾ in (2 cm):

Row 1: (K1, p1) across, end with k1.

Subsequent Rows: Work purl over knit and knit over purl.

At the same time: On 1st row, pm: Work 50 (54, 60, 62, 66, 70, 72) seed sts, pm, work 49 seed sts, pm, work 50 (54, 60, 62, 66, 70, 72) seed sts.

Change to larger-size circular. The 5 outermost sts at each side are edge sts and are worked in seed st throughout. The rest of the body is worked in stockinette but with the pattern following the chart between the 2 markers. See charts on page 88.

Continue in stockinette with pattern between the markers until body measures 4 (4¾, 5½, 6, 6¼, 7, 8) in [10 (12, 14, 15, 16, 18, 20) cm].

On the last row, RS, BO 6 sts at each side for the armholes as follows:

K34 (36, 39, 40, 42, 44, 45), BO 6 sts, k10 (12, 15, 16, 18, 20, 21), work 49 sts in charted pattern, k10 (12, 15, 16, 18, 20, 21), BO 6 sts, k34 (36, 39, 40, 42, 44, 45) sts.

Set body aside while you knit sleeves.

SLEEVES

With smaller-size dpn, CO 50 (50, 52,52, 54, 56, 56) sts. Divide sts onto dpn and join. Work around in seed st for ¾ in (2 cm).

Change to larger size needles. Always purl the 1st (marked) st for center of underarm.

The sleeve is worked in stockinette. When sleeve measures 1¼ in (3 cm), increase 1 st with M1 on each side of marked st (the purl st). Increase the same way every ¾ in (2 cm) until there are 60 (60, 66, 68, 72, 76, 76) sts.

Continue until sleeve measures 5¼ (6, 7, 8, 8¾, 9½, 9¾) in [13 (15, 18, 20, 22, 24, 25) cm] or desired length.

Next rnd: BO 6 sts centered on underarm. Set sleeve aside while you knit 2nd sleeve the same way.

Place sleeves on circular with body, matching underarms = 245 (253, 277, 285, 301, 317, 321) sts total.

Pm for raglan lines at each intersection of body and sleeve = 4 markers.

Continue in stockinette, with pattern between markers and seed st on the 5 outermost sts at each side.

The 1st row = WS.

Shape raglan, decreasing at each raglan marker as follows:

Work as est until 2 sts before next marker, sl 1, k1, psso, k2tog; rep * to * , across, ending with front as est to end of row = 8 sts decreased.

Note: If the decreases occur within the pattern, work affected pattern sts in stockinette.

Continue as est until you've decreased a total of 18 (18, 20, 21, 22, 24, 25) times.

Purl 1 row on WS. Knit 1 row, decreasing 10 sts evenly spaced across.

NECKBAND

Change to smaller-size circular, Work ¾ in (2 cm) in seed st and then BO in seed st.

With crochet hook, make 2 button loops at top of neck band on left side.

Attach yarn with 1 sl st in corner and ch 4. Attach chain with 1 sl st about ⅝ in (1.5 cm) lower on edge (so loop lies evenly between the edge sts). Work 4 sl sts along edge and then make another button loop. Finish with 1 sl st.

Abbreviations:

sl st = slip stitch
ch = chain stitch

FINISHING

Weave in all ends neatly on WS. Sew on 2 buttons.

Lay a damp towel over sweater and leave until dry or gently steam-press sweater under a damp pressing cloth.

Olivia Christening Dress

KlompeLompe's own christening dress is named for the most beautiful
Olivia, who wore it for her christening. We made two versions.
One was knitted with Merino wool in Putty and has leather cords
at the waist to make this dress tough-looking, but in an amazingly fine way.
The other was knitted with alpaca/silk and has a silk ribbon at the waist.
It's light and pretty for a more classic christening-dress look.

SIZES: One size

FINISHED MEASUREMENTS
Chest: Approx. 18¾ (47.5 cm)
Total Length: Approx. 31½ in (80 cm)

MATERIALS
YARN: Sandnes Garn KlompeLompe Tynn
Merinoull (fine Merino wool) [CYCA #1 –
fingering, 100% Merino wool, 191 yd (175 m)
/ 50 g]
or
Sandnes Garn Alpakka Silke [CYCA #1 –
fingering, 70% alpaca, 30% silk, 20% nylon,
219 yd (200 m) / 50 g]

YARN COLORS AND AMOUNTS:
1013 (Tynn Merino): 350 g or 1002 (Alpakka
Silke): 250 g
NEEDLES: US sizes 1.5 and 2.5 (2.5 and 3
mm): 16 and 24 in (40 and 60 cm) circulars
and sets of 5 dpn
CROCHET HOOK: US size D-3 (3 mm)
NOTIONS: 5 small buttons, length of ribbon or
leather cord for waist tie

GAUGE: 27 sts on larger-size needles = 4 in
(10 cm).
Adjust needle size to obtain correct gauge if
necessary.

The dress is worked from the top down,
beginning back and forth on a circular
needle.

With smaller-size circular, CO 72 sts, Work 4
rows back and forth in seed st:
Row 1: (K1, p1) across, end with k1.
Subsequent Rows: Work purl over knit and
knit over purl.

Change to larger-size circular and knit 1 row,
placing markers:
K13, pm, k10 (sleeve), pm, k26, pm, k10
(sleeve), pm, k13. Purl 1 row.

Continue in stockinette, increasing on RS
rows at each marker as follows:
Knit to st before marker, RLI, sl m, LLI = 8
sts increased. After increasing 15 times, knit
next row but move sleeve sts to a holder and
CO 8 new sts over gap = 128 sts. Now join to
knit in the round.

Knit 6 rnds, purl 1 rnd, knit 2 rnds.
Eyelet rnd: K3 k2tog, yo, *k6, k2tog, yo*; rep
* to * until 3 sts rem, k3.

Knit 2 rnds, purl 1 rnd, knit 1 rnd,
increasing 4 sts evenly spaced around.

Pm before knitting next rnd: 4 sts, pm, 25
sts (charted pattern), pm, 8 sts, pm, 25 sts,
(pattern), pm, 8 sts, pm, 25 sts (pattern), pm,
8 sts, pm, 25 sts (pattern), pm, 4 sts.

Now work following chart for the 4 pattern
sections and in stockinette for rem sts.

Following sequence below, increase (with
M1) 1 st on each side of the 4 center sts in
each stockinette section = 8 sts increased
per round. If desired, pm on each side of the
4 sts in each stockinette section.

Increase the 1st time when garment
measures ¾ in (2 cm) from rnd you purled
after the eyelet rnd and then every ¾ in (2
cm) until you've increased a total of 21 times
= 300 sts.

Continue without increasing until skirt
measures 26½ in (67 cm) from rnd you
purled after eyelet rnd. End with 4 rnds seed
st, binding off in seed st on last rnd.

SLEEVES
With larger size dpn, CO 4 sts. Work the 40
held sts and then CO 4 sts; pm.

Work around in stockinette. After 1½ in
(3.5 cm), decrease as follows: K1, k2tog, knit
until 3 sts before marker, sl 1, k1, psso, k1.
Decrease the same way every 1½ in (3.5 cm)
until 40 sts rem and sleeve measures 6¼ in
(16 cm). Knit 1 rnd, decreasing 6 sts evenly
spaced around. Change to smaller-size dpn
and work 4 rnds in seed st, binding off in
seed st on last rnd.

Make the 2nd sleeve the same way.

Crochet edging around neck: Work around
back neck opening with sc. Work 1 sl st
in each sc, making 5 buttonloops evenly
spaced on left side: ch 5 for each button loop
and then sl st into next sc.

Abbreviations:
sc = single crochet
sl st = slip stitch

FINISHING
Weave in all ends neatly on WS.
Block dress by laying a damp towel over it
and leaving it until completely dry or gently

steam-press under a damp pressing cloth.
Do not steam-press seed stitch bands, since
that might cause the bands to roll up.

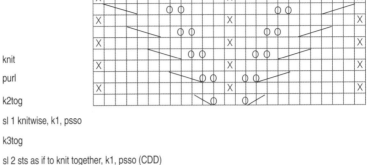

	knit
X	purl
	k2tog
	sl 1 knitwise, k1, psso
	k3tog
	sl 2 sts as if to knit together, k1, psso (CDD)
	yo between 2 sts

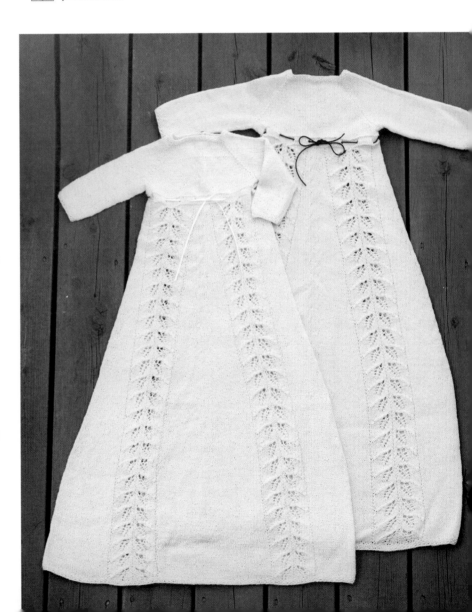

Olivia Christening Cap

A pretty bonnet with delicate lace leaves to match
the christening dress. The cap can, of course, be worn
for everyday and would be lovely in other colors.

SIZES: 0–1 (3, 6–12) months

MATERIALS

YARN: Sandnes Garn KlompeLompe Tynn Merinoull (fine Merino wool) [CYCA #1 – fingering, 100% Merino wool, 191 yd (175 m) / 50 g]

YARN COLORS AND AMOUNTS:
4032: 50 (50, 50) g

NEEDLES: US sizes 1.5 and 2.5 (2.5 and 3 mm): 16 in (40 cm) circulars and set of 5 dpn in larger size

CROCHET HOOK: US size D-3 (3 mm)

NOTIONS: length of ribbon or leather cord for ties

GAUGE: 27 sts on larger-size needles = 4 in (10 cm).
Adjust needle size to obtain correct gauge if necessary.

• •

With smaller-size circular, CO 75 (81, 85) sts. Work 4 rows back and forth in seed st:
Row 1: (K1, p1) across, end with k1.
Subsequent Rows: Work purl over knit and knit over purl.

Place markers before knitting next row:
2 sts, pm, 21 sts (charted pattern), pm, 4 (7, 9) sts, pm, 21 sts (charted pattern), pm, 4 (7, 9) sts, pm, 21 sts (charted pattern), pm, 2 sts.

Change to larger-size circular.
    Work in stockinette except for the 3 pattern sections, which are worked following chart A.
    After working chart 3 (4, 5) times, join to begin working in the round.

Continue in pattern and stockinette as est.
    Work 3 rnds.

Next (decrease) rnd: K2, *21 sts pattern, sl 1, k1, psso, k0 (3, 5), k2tog*; rep * to * once more, 21 sts pattern, k2.

Work 2 rnds without decreasing.
Next (decrease) rnd: K2, *21 sts pattern, k0 (3, 5), k0 (k2tog, k2tog)*; rep * to * once more, 21 sts pattern, k2.

Work 2 rnds without decreasing and then begin chart B pattern on the 2nd rnd.

Size 0–1 month: Next (decrease) rnd: K2tog, *21 sts pattern, k2*; rep * to * once more, 21 sts pattern, sl 1, k1, psso.

Size 3 months: Next (decrease) rnd: K2tog, *21 sts pattern, sl 1, k1, psso, k2tog*; rep * to * once more, 21 sts pattern, sl 1, k1, psso.

Size 6–12 months: Next (decrease) rnd: K2tog, *21 sts pattern, sl 1, k1, psso, k2tog, k2tog*; rep * to * once more, 21 sts pattern, sl 1, k1, psso.

All sizes: Work 1 rnd without decreasing.

Decrease in pattern as indicated on chart B, working rem sts in stockinette.

After completing chart B, work k2tog around, ending with k1.

Cut yarn and draw end through rem sts; tighten.

With RS facing, pick up and knit about 59 (67, 73) sts for cord casing along neck edge.
    Work 12 rows back and forth in seed st; BO in seed st on row 13. Fold edging in half and sew down on WS. Thread cord through casing.

Chart A

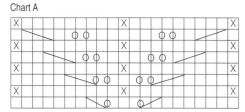

Chart B

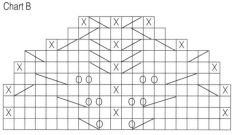

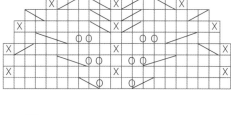

	knit on RS, purl on WS
X	purl on RS, knit on WS
	k2tog
	sl 1 knitwise, k1, psso
	k3tog
	sl 2 sts as if to knit together, k1, psso (CDD)
	yo between 2 sts

Summer

Balloon Rompers

A sweet and comfy pair of summer rompers.
So nice with bare feet and sun-warmed skin, but the garment can
also be worn with tights and a thin undershirt on colder days.

SIZES: 0 (1–2, 3, 6, 9, 12, 18, 24, 36) months

FINISHED MEASUREMENTS
Chest: Approx. 19¾ (21, 22, 23¼, 24½, 25½, 28, 29¼, 30¼) in [50 (53, 56, 59, 62, 65, 71, 74, 77 cm]
Total length excluding straps: Approx. 8¼ (8¾, 10¼, 10¾, 11, 11¾, 13½, 14½, 15½) in [21 (22.5, 26, 27, 28, 30, 34, 37, 39) cm]

MATERIALS
YARN: Sandnes Garn KlompeLompe Tynn Merinoull (fine Merino wool) [CYCA #1 – fingering, 100% Merino wool, 191 yd (175 m) / 50 g]
YARN COLORS AND AMOUNTS:
Color 4331: 50 (100, 100, 100, 100, 100, 150, 150, 150) g
NEEDLES: US sizes 1.5 and 2.5 (2.5 and 3 mm): 16 in (40 cm) circulars and sets of 5 dpn

GAUGE: 27 sts on larger-size needles = 4 in (10 cm).
Adjust needle size to obtain correct gauge if necessary.

With smaller-size circular, CO 114 (120, 126, 130, 134, 144, 154, 154, 154) sts. Join, being careful not to twist cast-on row; pm for beginning of rnd. Work 6 (8, 8, 10, 10, 10, 10, 10, 10 rnds k1 p1 ribbing. Change to larger- size circular and knit 1 rnd.

Purl 1 rnd, increasing 22 (24, 26, 30, 34, 32, 38, 46, 54) sts evenly spaced around = 136 (144, 152, 160, 168, 176, 192, 200, 208) sts.

Raise the back with short row. **Note:** Before each turn, make a yarnover and then turn. When you later come to the yo, k/p the yarnover together with the following st):

SIZE 0 MONTHS:
P15; turn, k30; turn, p40; turn, k50; turn, p60, p25.

SIZES 1–2 (3, 6, 9, 12) MONTHS:
P15; turn, k30; turn, p40; turn, k50; turn, p60; turn, k70; turn, p35.

SIZES 18 (24, 36) MONTHS:
P15; turn, k30; turn, p40; turn, k50; turn, p60; turn, k70; turn, p80; turn, k90, p45.

You should now be at the beginning of the rnd.

Pattern (rep to specified length):
Rnd 1: *P3, k2, p3*; rep * to * around.
Rnd 2: *P3, sl 2, p3*; rep * to * around.
Rnd 3: *P3, k2, p3*; rep * to * around.
Rnd 4: *P3, sl 2, p3*; rep * to * around.
Rnd 5: *P2, RC, LC, p2*; rep * to * around.
Rnd 6: *P2, sl 1, p2, sl 1, p2*; rep * to * around.
Rnd 7: *P1, RC, p2, LC, p1*; rep * to * around.
Rnd 8: *P1, sl 1, p4, sl 1, p1*; rep * to * around.
Rnd 9: RC, p4, LC*; rep * to * around.
Rnd 10: *Sl 1, p6, sl 1*; rep * to * around.
Rnd 11: *K1, p6, k1*; rep * to * around.
Rnd 12: *Sl 1, p6, sl 1*; rep * to * around.
Rnd 13: *K1, p6, k1*; rep * to * around.
Rnd 14: *Sl 1, p6, sl 1*; rep * to * around.
Rnd 15: *LC, p4, RC*; rep * to * around.
Rnd 16: *P1, sl 1, p4, sl 1, p1*; rep * to * around.
Rnd 17: *P1, LC, p2, RC, p1*; rep * to * around.
Rnd 18: *P2, sl 1, p2, sl 1, p2*; rep * to * around.
Rnd 19: *P2, LC, RC, p2*; rep * to * around.
Rnd 20: *P3, sl 2, p3*; rep * to * around.

RS = RIGHT CROSS
Method 1: Skip 1st st but leave it on needle, knit 2nd st in front of 1st st and then purl 1st st.
Method 2: Place 1st st on cable needle and hold in back of work. Knit 2nd st and then purl st on cable needle.

LC = LEFT CROSS
Method 1: Skip 1st st but leave it on needle, purl 2nd st behind 1st st and then knit 1st st.
Method 2: Place 1st st on cable needle and hold in front of work. Purl 2nd st (behind st on cable needle) and then knit st on cable needle.

Continue in pattern until body measures approx. 5½ (6, 6¼, 6¾, 7½, 8¼, 9, 9½, 10¼) in [14 (15, 16, 17, 19, 21, 23, 24, 26) cm] in front and you've just finished with a partial round in the pattern, work the next rnd as follows:
    Cut yarn, move the 1st 16 (18, 19, 21, 21, 22, 22, 24, 25) sts to right needle on the next row. Begin working from this point.

BO 40 (40, 43, 44, 48, 50, 58, 58, 60) sts, work 24 (28, 28, 30, 30, 32, 32, 36, 38) sts in pattern (front), BO 40 (40, 43, 44, 48, 50, 58, 58, 60) sts.
Work in pattern, binding off purlwise the rem 32 (26, 38, 42, 42, 44, 44, 48 50) sts (back).

The back is now worked separately, back and forth. Note that the partial rows (WS) in pattern are knitted when it says purl and slipped where it says slip st. In that case, let yarn lie on WS of work.

For example: Rnd 2: *K3, sl 2 with yarn in front, k3*: rep * to *around.

Each time you are on the WS, decrease 1 st at each side with k2tog at beginning and k2tog at end of row.
    Note that the pattern gradually disappears at each side, and there will be some rows beginning with 1 more purl on the RS than is usual.

Rep the decreases on every WS row until 22 (26, 26, 38, 28, 30, 30, 34, 36) sts rem.
    On the next row (RS), BO rem sts.

Make the front the same way. The 1st row is WS.
    Decrease until 22 (26, 26, 38, 28, 30, 30, 34, 36) sts rem. Work 8 (8, 8, 8, 8, 10, 10, 10, 10) rows without decreasing at the sides. BO on next, RS, row.

Seam front and back with mattress st (see page 124). Seam crotch (bound-off sts on front and back).

With smaller-size circular, pick up and knit sts for ribbing round each leg. Pick up about 3 sts for every sts/rows. Join and work 6 (6, 6, 6, 8, 8, 8, 8) rnds k1, p1 ribbing; BO in ribbing on last rnd.

Now make the bib on the front. With RS facing and larger-size circular, pick up and knit 38 (40, 42, 44, 50, 54, 58, 58, 58) sts centered on front in ribbing. The bib is worked back and forth in stockinette.
    Work 3 rows. On the next (RS) row, decrease as follows:
    K1, k2tog, knit until 3 sts rem, sl 1, k1, psso, k1.

Rep the decrease row every 4th row a total of 4 (4, 5, 5, 6, 6, 7, 7, 8) times.
Purl 1 row. Change to smaller-size needle and BO rather firmly with I-cord bind-off method (I-cord: see page 127).

I-cord BO: CO 3 sts, slip the 3 sts to left needle.
    K2 and then k2tog tbl. Slip the 3 sts to left needle.
    Rep * to *. When 3 sts rem, cut yarn and draw end through rem sts.

Now edge bib sides with I-cord and make ties. Use smaller-size dpn.
    Begin on left side. CO 3 sts. With RS facing, pick up and knit 1 st in each st along left edge of bib.
    Cut yarn and bind off with I-Cord BO on RS. When 3 sts rem, continue in I-cord until tie measures approx. 6 in (15 cm) long.

On right side of bib, begin by making the tie. Leave last 3 sts on needle. With RS facing, pick up and knit sts along right side of bib. Cut yarn and work I-cord BO where you began with sts from the tie.

Finally, make the back. It is worked as for the bib, but now you should pick up and knit 28 (30, 32, 34, 40, 44, 48, 48, 48) sts centered on back. Decrease a total of 5 (5, 6, 6, 7, 7, 8, 8, 9) times before you bind off bib.

FINISHING
Weave in all ends neatly on WS. Sew ends of I-cords as invisibly as possible to ribbing on body.
Lay a damp towel over rompers and leave until dry or gently steam-press under a damp pressing cloth.

Top left: Color 434 ──≫

Lilly Baby Socks

Charming socks in our Lilly pattern. These socks stay on baby's feet well and have a smart tie to hold them in place.

Level 2

SIZES: 1–3 (6–9, 12–18 months, 2, 3–4 years)

MATERIALS

YARN: Sandnes Garn KlompeLompe Tynn Merinoull (fine Merino wool) [CYCA #1 – fingering, 100% Merino wool, 191 yd (175 m) / 50 g]

YARN COLORS AND AMOUNTS:
Color 1013: 50 (50, 50, 50, 50) g

NEEDLES: US size 1.5 (2.5 mm): set of 5 dpn or use 32 in (80 cm) circular for magic loop (see video on magic loop technique on klompelompe.no).

NOTIONS: Length of faux leather cord if not using twisted yarn cord for sock ties

GAUGE: 32 sts = 4 in (10 cm).
Adjust needle size to obtain correct gauge if necessary.

The round begins at center back.
CO 40 (44, 48, 52, 56) sts. Divide sts onto dpn and join. Work around in k2, p2 ribbing for 2½ (3, 3¼, 3¾, 4, 4) in [6.5 (7.5, 8.5, 9.5, 10, 10) cm].

On the next rnd, work eyelets:
Sizes 1–3 and 12–18 months, 3–4 years: *K2tog, yo, p2* rep * to * around.
Sizes 6–9 months and 2 years: *K2tog, yo, p2*; rep * to * 5 (6) times, k2, p2; rep * to * 5 (6) times.

Work 3 (4, 5, 5, 6) more rnds in ribbing.

Cut yarn. Place the back 20 (20, 24, 24, 28) sts on 1 needle = 10 (10, 12, 12, 14) sts on each side.

Knitting Tip: If you are working with magic loop, you can leave the front sts on 1 part of the needle cord, while you work the heel back and forth on the other part of needle.

Work heel on back sts as follows:

HEEL SHAPING
The heel is worked back and forth in stockinette.
  Row 1 (RS): Knit until 1 st rem; turn.
  Row 2 (WS): Sl 1 purlwise, tighten yarn and purl until 1 st rem; turn.
  Row 3 (RS): Sl 1 knitwise, tighten yarn and knit until 2 sts rem; turn.
  Row 4 (WS): Sl purlwise, tighten yarn, purl until 2 sts rem; turn.
  Continue decreasing the same way, with 1 more st rem each time, until 8 (8, 10, 10, 12) sts rem at center of needle; pm. Continue working back and forth but now add 1 more st on each row. To avoid holes at the transition: Lift strand between sts (before the st to be added) and place twisted on needle. Knit strand together with st. Work back and forth, adding 1 more st each row until working all heel sts.

Now work in the round; rnd begins at side, before heel.

Knit 1 rnd, adjusting st count to 41 (41, 47, 51, 55) sts = 21 (21, 21, 25, 25) sts for front (instep) and rem sts for back.

Before beginning next rnd, lift strand before 1st st and twist onto needle; knit strand tog with 1st st to avoid a hole at beginning of rnd.

The back continues in stockinette, and the instep is worked in lace pattern following chart.

After working charted rows 2 (2.5, 3, 3.5, 4) times, knit 1 rnd and then decrease 1 st at front = 40 (40, 46, 50, 54) sts rem. Move side markers so that you have the same number of sts each for sole and instep.

Shape toe on sole and instep as follows:
Rnd 1: *K1, sl 1, k1, psso, knit until 3 sts rem before side marker, k2tog, k1*; rep * to * = 4 sts decreased on rnd.
Rnd 2: Knit.
Rep Rnds 1–2 a total of 5 (5, 6, 6, 7) times = 20 (20, 22, 26, 26) sts rem.

Make second sock the same way.

FINISHING
Cut yarn, leaving long end to sew up with.
Lay sock flat and sew the 10 (10, 11, 13, 13) sts of instep to the 10 (10, 11, 13, 13) sts of sole with mattress st.
Weave in all ends neatly on WS.

Place damp towel on socks and leave until completely dry.
Thread a twisted yarn or faux leather cord though eyelet rnd on each sock.

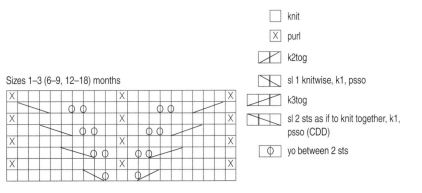

	knit
X	purl
⟋	k2tog
⟍	sl 1 knitwise, k1, psso
⟋	k3tog
⟍	sl 2 sts as if to knit together, k1, psso (CDD)
Ⓞ	yo between 2 sts

Sizes 1–3 (6–9, 12–18) months

Sizes 2 (3-4) years

Randi Pullover for Children

A simple summer pullover knitted in a cool yarn.
The front is worked in double seed stitch
while the back and sleeves are in stockinette.

SIZES: 6 months (1, 2, 4, 6, 8, 10, 12, 14 years)

FINISHED MEASUREMENTS
Chest: Approx. 20½ (22, 23¾, 25¼, 26¾, 26¾, 28¼, 30, 31½) in [52 (56, 60, 64, 68, 68, 72, 76, 80) cm]
Total Length: Approx.12¾ (13¾, 14¼, 15½, 16¼, 17¾, 18½, 19¾, 21¾) in [32 (35, 36, 39, 41, 45, 47, 50, 55) cm]

MATERIALS
YARN: Sandnes Garn Line [CYCA #4 - worsted, Afghan, Aran, 55% cotton, 33% rayon, 14% linen, 120 yd (110 m) / 50 g]
YARN COLORS AND AMOUNTS:
Color 4621: 150 (150, 200, 200, 200, 250, 250, 300, 300) g
NEEDLES: US size 6 (4 mm): 24 and 32 in (60 and 80 cm) circulars and set of 5 dpn or use 32 in (80 cm) circular for magic loop (see video on magic loop technique on klompelompe.no).

GAUGE: 20 sts = 4 in (10 cm).
Adjust needle size to obtain correct gauge if necessary.

The sweater is worked in the round on a circular needle, from the bottom up.

With circular, CO 104 (112, 120, 128 136, 136, 144, 152, 160) sts. Join, being careful not to twist cast-on row. Pm for beginning of rnd and at side with 52 (56, 60, 64, 68, 68, 72, 76, 80) sts each for front and back.

Work around in k1, p1 ribbing for 1¼ in (3 cm).

Double Seed St:
Rows 1–2: *K2, p2*; rep * to *.
Rows 3–4: *P2, k2*; rep * to *.
Rep Rows 1–4 for pattern.

Now work around with front in double seed st and back in stockinette (knit all rnds).
When body measures 8¼ (8¾, 9½, 10¼, 11, 11¾, 12¾, 13¾, 15) in [21 (22, 24, 26, 28, 30, 32, 35, 38) cm], BO 8 sts at each side (= BO 4 sts before each marker and 4 sts after each marker).

Set body aside while you knit sleeves.

SLEEVES
With dpn, CO 34 (36, 36, 36 38, 38, 40, 40, 42) sts. Divide sts onto dpn and join.
Work around in k1, p1 ribbing for ⅝ in (1.5 cm). The sleeves are worked in stockinette. The 1st st is a marked st for center of underarm.

When sleeve is 1¼ in (3 cm) long, increase 1 st with M1 on each side of marked st. Increase the same way every ⅜ (⅜, ⅜, ⅝, ¾, ¾, ¾, ¾, 1) in [1 (1, 1, 1.5, 2, 2, 2, 2, 2.5) cm] until there are 50 (52, 52, 54, 54, 56, 56, 58, 58) sts.

Continue in stockinette until sleeve is 4¼ (5¼, 6, 7, 8, 8¾, 9½, 9¾, 10¾) in [11 (13, 15, 18, 20, 22, 24, 25, 27) cm] long.

Next Rnd: BO 4 sts, knit until 4 sts rem, BO 4 sts.

Set 1st sleeve aside while you knit 2nd sleeve the same way.

JOIN BODY AND SLEEVES
Arrange sleeves on circular with body, matching underarms = 172 (184, 192, 204, 212, 216, 224, 236, 244) sts total. The rnd now begins at beginning of left sleeve.
Pm at each intersection between body and sleeve. Always knit the st before and after each marker. Work 5 rnds with back and sleeves in stockinette and front in double seed st.

Begin raglan shaping:
Decrease rnd: K1, k2tog, *work until 3 sts before marker, k2tog tbl, k2, k2tog*; rep * to * to last marker, k2tog tbl, k1.

Decrease the same way on every other rnd a total of 12 (13, 14, 15, 16, 17, 18, 19, 19) times = 76 (80, 80, 84, 84, 80, 80, 84, 92) sts rem.

Work around in k1, p1 ribbing for 1¼ in (3 cm). BO in ribbing.

FINISHING
Seam underarms.
Weave in all ends neatly on WS.
Place damp towel on sweater and leave until completely dry.

Randi Pullover for Adults

A summer pullover for Mom. Knitted in lovely yarn,
it's perfect for a warm summer day.

SIZES: XS (S, M, L, XL)

FINISHED MEASUREMENTS
Chest: Approx. 33½ (35½, 37, 43¼, 45¾) in
[85 (90, 94, 110, 116) cm]
Total Length: Approx. 23 (23¾, 24¾, 26¾,
28) in [58 (60, 63, 68, 71) cm]

MATERIALS
YARN: Sandnes Garn Line [CYCA #4 –
worsted, Afghan, Aran, 55% cotton, 33%
rayon, 14% linen, 120 yd (110 m) / 50 g]
YARN COLORS AND AMOUNTS:
Color 6554: 350 (400, 450, 550, 600) g
NEEDLES: US size 6 (4 mm): 24 and 32 in
(60 and 80 cm) circulars and set of 5 dpn
or use 32 in (80 cm) circular for magic loop
(see video on magic loop technique on
klompelompe.no).

GAUGE: 20 sts = 4 in (10 cm).
Adjust needle size to obtain correct gauge
if necessary.

The sweater is worked in the round on a
circular needle, from the bottom up.

With circular, CO 168 (180, 188, 220 232) sts.
Join, being careful not to twist cast-on row.
Pm for beginning of rnd and at side with 84
(90, 94, 110, 116) sts each for front and back.

Work around in k1, p1 ribbing for 2 in (5 cm).

DOUBLE SEED ST:
Rows 1–2: *K2, p2*; rep * to *. End with k0
(2, 2, 2, 0),
Rows 3–4: *P2, k2*; rep * to *. End with p0
(2, 2, 2, 0).
Rep Rows 1–4 for pattern.

Now work around with front in double seed st
and back in stockinette (knit all rnds).
    When body measures 16½ (17¼, 18¼, 19,
19¾) in [42 (44, 46, 48, 50) cm], BO 8 sts at
each side (= BO 4 sts before each marker
and 4 sts after each marker).

Set body aside while you knit sleeves.

SLEEVES
With dpn, CO 44 (48, 52, 54, 58) sts. Divide
sts onto dpn and join.
Work around in k1, p1 ribbing for ¾ in (2 cm).
The sleeves are worked in stockinette. The
1st st is a marked st for center of underarm.

When sleeve is 1¼ in (3 cm) long, increase
1 st with M1 on each side of marked st.
Increase the same way every 1⅜ (1½, 1½,
1¼, 1½) in [3.5 (4, 4, 3, 4) cm] until there are
58 (60, 64, 70, 76) sts.

Continue in stockinette until sleeve is 11¾ in
(30 cm) long or desired length.
    Next rnd: BO 4 sts, knit until 4 sts rem,
BO 4 sts.

Set 1st sleeve aside while you knit 2nd
sleeve the same way.

JOIN BODY AND SLEEVES
Arrange sleeves on circular with body,
matching underarms = 252 (268, 284,
328, 352) sts total. The rnd now begins at
beginning of left sleeve.
    Pm at each intersection between body
and sleeve. Always knit the st before and
after each marker. Work 5 rnds with back
and sleeves in stockinette and front in
double seed st.

Begin raglan shaping:
Decrease rnd: K1, k2tog, *work until 3 sts
before marker, k2tog tbl, k2, k2tog*; rep * to *
to last marker, k2tog tbl, k1.

Decrease the same way on every other rnd
a total of 18 (19, 21, 26, 29) times = 108 (116,
116, 120, 120) sts rem.

Work around in k1, p1 ribbing for 1¼ in (3
cm). BO in ribbing.

FINISHING
Seam underarms.
Weave in all ends neatly on WS.
Place damp towel on sweater and leave until
completely dry.

Summer-
Sweet Skirt
for Children

SIZES: 2 (4, 6, 8, 10, 12–14) years

FINISHED MEASUREMENTS

Waist (without elastic): Approx. 21¾ (21¾, 22½, 24, 24¾, 24¾) in [55.5 (55.5, 57.5, 61, 63, 63) cm]

Length: 8 (8¾, 9½, 9¾, 11, 12½) in [20 (22, 24, 25, 28, 31) cm]

MATERIALS

YARN: Sandnes Garn KlompeLompe Tynn Merinoull (fine Merino wool) [CYCA #1 – fingering, 100% Merino wool, 191 yd (175 m) / 50 g]

YARN COLOR AND AMOUNTS:

Color 7251: 150 (150, 150, 150, 200, 200) g

NEEDLES: US sizes 1.5 and 2.5 (2.5 and 3 mm): 16 and 24 in (40 and 60 cm) circulars

NOTIONS: waistband elastic: to fit around waist + seam allowance; leather belt to fit waist

GAUGE: 27 sts on larger-size needle = 4 in (10 cm).

Adjust needle size to obtain correct gauge if necessary.

The skirt begins at the waist and is knitted in the round on a circular needle.

With smaller-size circular, CO 150 (150, 155, 165, 170, 170) sts. Join, being careful not to twist cast-on row; pm for beginning of rnd. Work around in stockinette for 1¾ in (4.5 cm).

   Next rnd (foldline): *K2tog, yo*; rep * to * around.

Work around in stockinette for 1¾ in (4.5 cm).

Change to larger-size circular.

Increase Rnd 1: *K5, M1*; rep * to * around = 180 (180, 186, 198, 204, 204) sts.

Work 1¼ in (3 cm) in stockinette.

Increase Rnd 2: *K6, M1*; rep * to * around = 210 (210, 217, 231, 238, 238) sts.

Work 2 in (5 cm) in stockinette.

Increase Rnd 3: *K7, M1*; rep * to * around = 240 (240, 248, 264, 272, 272) sts.

Continue in stockinette until skirt measures 8 (8¾, 9½, 9¾, 11, 12½) in [20 (22, 24, 25, 28, 31) cm] from foldline.

Now work around in garter st (= alternate knit 1 rnd, purl 1 rnd) until skirt measures 10¼ (11, 11¾, 12¾, 13¾, 15) in [26 (28, 30, 32, 35, 38) cm] from foldline. BO.

   Fold waistband at eyelet rnd (foldline) and sew down on back. Insert waistband elastic and finish sewing down band.

FINISHING

Weave in all ends neatly on WS.

Gently steam-press skirt under damp pressing cloth.

BELT LOOPS

Make 5 belt loops:

   With smaller-size needle, CO 7 sts. Work back and forth in k1, p1 ribbing for 1¾ in (4.5 cm). BO in ribbing.

   Sew on the loops evenly spaced around, with 1 at center back.

Use a leather belt or something similar around waist.

Summer-Sweet Skirt for Adults

The ultimate "knitting night" project. Perfect to have with you on a visit, or to knit while you watch your favorite TV series. The skirt has a classic silhouette and mother and daughter can have matching skirts. Perhaps Grandma would like one too?

SIZES: XS (S, M, L, XL)

FINISHED MEASUREMENTS
Waist (without elastic): Approx. 26½ (27¼, 27¾, 30¾, 33½) in [67 (69, 70.5, 78, 85) cm]
Length: 22½ (22¾, 23¼, 23¾, 23¾) in [57 (58, 59, 60, 60) cm]

MATERIALS
YARN: Sandnes Garn KlompeLompe Tynn Merinoull (fine Merino wool) [CYCA #1 – fingering, 100% Merino wool, 191 yd (175 m) / 50 g]
YARN COLORS AND AMOUNTS:
Color 6061: 250 (350, 350, 350, 350) g
NEEDLES: US sizes 1.5 and 2.5 (2.5 and 3 mm): 24 in (60 cm) circulars
NOTIONS: waistband elastic: to fit around waist + seam allowance; leather belt to fit waist

GAUGE: 27 sts on larger-size needle = 4 in (10 cm).
Adjust needle size to obtain correct gauge if necessary.

The skirt begins at the waist and is knitted in the round on a circular needle.

With smaller-size circular, CO 180 (185, 190, 210, 230) sts. Join, being careful not to twist cast-on row; pm for beginning of rnd. Work around in stockinette for 1¾ in (4.5 cm).
    Next rnd (foldline): *K2tog, yo*; rep * to * around, ending with k0 (1, 0, 0 , 0).
Work around in stockinette for 1¾ in (4.5 cm).

Change to larger-size circular.
Increase Rnd 1: *K5, M1*; rep * to * around = 216 (222, 228, 252, 276) sts.
Work 2 in (5 cm) in stockinette.
Increase Rnd 2: *K6, M1*; rep * to * around = 252 (252, 259, 266, 294, 322) sts.
Work 3¼ in (8 cm) in stockinette.
Increase Rnd 3: *K7, M1*; rep * to * around = 288 (296, 304, 336, 368) sts.
Continue in stockinette until skirt measures 19¼ (19¾, 20, 20½, 20½) in [49 (50, 51, 52, 52) cm] from foldline.

Now work around in garter st (= alternate knit 1 rnd, purl 1 rnd) until skirt measures 22½ (22¾, 23¼, 23¾, 23¾) in [57 (58, 59, 60, 60) cm from foldline. BO.

Fold waistband at eyelet rnd (foldline) and sew down on back. Insert waistband elastic and finish sewing down band.

FINISHING
Weave in all ends neatly on WS.
Gently steam-press skirt under damp pressing cloth.

BELT LOOPS
Make 5 belt loops:
    With smaller-size needle, CO 7 sts. Work back and forth in k1, p1 ribbing for 1¾ in (4.5 cm). BO in ribbing.
    Sew on the loops evenly spaced around, with 1 at center back.
Use a leather belt or something similar around waist.

Block-Pattern Shorts

Shorts for warmer days knitted in a wool-cotton blend yarn. Make a solid-color version or combine different bold colors for the shorts and drawstring.

With smaller-size circular, CO 98 (108, 112, 120, 128) sts. Join, being careful not to twist cast-on row; pm for beginning of rnd.

Knit 9 rnds, purl 1 rnd, knit 4 rnds.
Next rnd: K43 (47, 49, 53, 57), k2tog, yo, k8 (10, 10, 10, 10), yo, sl 1, k1, psso, k43 (47, 49, 53, 57). Knit 5 rnds.

Change to larger-size circular.
Knit 1 rnd, increasing 14 (12, 16, 16, 8) sts evenly spaced around = 112 (120, 128, 136, 136) sts.

Raise back with short rows:
K10; turn, yo. P20; turn, yo and knit until 4 sts past previous turn (joining yo and next st with k2tog). Turn, yo, purl until 4 sts after previous turn.

Continue the same way until you've turned 3 (4, 4, 5, 5) times on each side. Knit to beginning of rnd.

Now work in pattern following chart until piece measures 3½ (4, 4¼, 4¾, 5½) in [9 (10, 11, 12, 14) cm] from rnd where you changed to larger-size needle.

Pm on each side of the center 7 sts at front and back (these 7 sts will form the crotch).
Increase 1 st with M1 on each side of the 7 marked st on front and back.
Increase the same way on every 3rd rnd a total of 4 (5, 5, 5, 5) times. On the last rnd, BO the 7 crotch sts at center front and back.

Knitting Tip
The pattern will not work out evenly as you increase. Do not work the 7 front and back sts in pattern. BO these sts after completing increases.

LEGS
Divide sts of 1 leg onto dpn; pm at beginning of rnd. With larger-size needles, work in the round.

Work 2 (2, 4, 4, 6) rnds in pattern. Change to smaller-size dpn and work in k1, p1 ribbing: on the 1st rnd, decrease 1 st at beginning of rnd. Work a total of 4 rnds in ribbing. BO in ribbing.

Work 2nd leg the same way.

FINISHING
Seam the crotch between front and back.
Fold down facing for waistband. Seam elastic and insert it into waistband casing. Sew down casing on WS.
Twist a cord drawstring to insert through waistband. Add tassels.

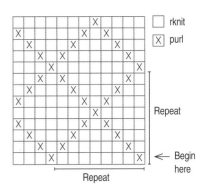

Color 3543 ⟶⟩⟩

Theodor Pullover

A favorite sweater to wear for everyday and parties. The buttoned neck opening and the classic stripe pattern make this a fun project to knit.

SIZES: 6 months (9, 12, 18 months, 2, 4, 6, 8, 10, 12, 14 years)

FINISHED MEASUREMENTS
Chest: Approx. 19¾ (20, 21¼, 21¾, 23¼, 24½, 26½, 29½, 30¾, 32, 33½) in [50 (51, 54, 55.5, 59, 62, 67.5, 75, 78, 81.5, 85) cm]
Total Length: Approx.10¼ (11, 12¼, 13½, 13¾, 14½, 17¼, 18½, 20½, 21¼, 22¾) in [26 (28, 31, 34, 35, 37, 44, 47, 52, 54, 58) cm]

MATERIALS
YARN: Sandnes Garn KlompeLompe Tynn Merinoull (fine Merino wool) [CYCA #1 – fingering, 100% Merino wool, 191 yd (175 m) / 50 g]
YARN COLORS AND AMOUNTS:
Color A 1013: 100 (100, 100, 100, 100, 150, 150, 100, 200, 200, 200) g
Color B 7251: 50 (100, 100, 100, 100, 100, 100, 100, 150, 150, 150) g
NEEDLES: US size 1.5 and 2.5 (2.5 and 3 mm): 16 and 24 in (40 and 60 cm) circulars and sets of 5 dpn or use 32 in (80 cm) circular for magic loop (see video on magic loop technique on klompelompe.no).
NOTIONS: 6 (6, 6, 6, 6, 8, 8, 8, 8, 8, 8) buttons

GAUGE: 27 sts on larger-size needles = 4 in (10 cm).
Adjust needle size to obtain correct gauge if necessary.

The sweater is worked in the round on a circular needle, from the bottom up.

With smaller-size circular and color A, CO 134 (138, 146, 150, 160, 168, 182, 202, 210, 220, 230) sts. Join, being careful not to twist cast-on row; pm for beginning of rnd.

Work around in k1, p1 ribbing for 1 (1, 1¼, 1¼, 1¼, 1¼, 1¼, 1⅜, 1⅜, 1⅜, 1⅜) in [2.5 (2.5, 3, 3, 3, 3, 3, 3.5, 3.5, 3.5, 3.5) cm].
Change to larger-size circular and color B. Begin stripe sequence: 4 rnds color B, 4 rnds color A.
Continue in stripe pattern until body measures 7½ (8¼, 9, 9¾, 10¼, 11, 12¾, 13¾, 15, 15¾, 16½) in [19 (21, 23, 25, 26, 28, 32, 35, 38, 40, 42) cm] and you have worked 3 rnds of a stripe. BO 8 sts centered on each side on the next rnd (last rnd of stripe) = 118 (122, 130, 134, 144, 152, 166, 186, 194, 204, 214) sts rem. Set body aside while you knit sleeves.

SLEEVES
With smaller-size dpn and color A, CO 38 (40, 40, 40, 42, 42, 52, 52, 56, 56, 56) sts. Divide sts onto dpn and join.
Work around in k1, p1 ribbing for 1 (1, 1¼, 1¼, 1¼, 1¼, 1¼, 1⅜, 1⅜, 1⅜, 1⅜) in [2.5 (2.5, 3, 3, 3, 3, 3, 3.5, 3.5, 3.5, 3.5) cm].
Begin stripe sequence. Measure 5½ (6¼, 7, 8, 9½, 10¾, 11¾, 12¾, 13½, 14¼, 15¾) in [14 (16, 18, 20, 24, 27, 30, 32, 34, 36, 40) cm] from top down on body to determine which color to begin stripes with after ribbing on

sleeve. This way, you'll match sleeves and body on the same rnd when you join the pieces for the yoke.
Change to larger size dpn. Shape sleeve (see Note below) and work in stripe pattern until sleeve is 5½ (6¼, 7, 8, 9½, 10¾, 11¾, 12¾, 13½, 14¼, 15¾) in [14 (16, 18, 20, 24, 27, 30, 32, 34, 36, 40) cm] from rnd where you changed needle size.
Note: after 2 rnds, begin shaping sleeve, increasing with M1:
K1, M1, knit until 1 st rem, M1, k1.
Increase the same way every 1 (1¼, 1¼,1⅜, 1½, 1½, 1¾, 1¾, 1¾, 2, 1¾) in [2.5 (3, 3, 3.5, 4, 4, 4.5, 4.5, 4.5, 5, 4.5) cm until there are 48 (48, 50, 50, 52, 54, 64, 66, 70, 70, 72) sts.
BO 8 sts centered on underarm on last rnd = 40 (40, 42, 42, 44, 46, 56, 58, 62, 62, 64) sts.

Set 1st sleeve aside while you knit 2nd sleeve the same way.

JOIN BODY AND SLEEVES
Arrange sleeves on larger-size circular with body, matching underarms = 198 (202, 214, 218, 232, 244, 278, 302, 318 28, 342) sts total. Pm at each intersection between body and sleeve. The rnd now begins at beginning of right sleeve.
Knit 2 rnds in stripe pattern.
Sizes 12 (14) years: Knit for ⅜ (¾) in [1 (2) cm].

With color A and smaller-size circular, with RS facing, pick up and knit sts along side of front for button bands.

Work 6 rows in k1, p1 ribbing, and, on Row 2, make 2 (2, 2, 2, 2, 3, 3, 3, 3, 3, 3) buttonholes. Note that buttonhole #3 (3, 3, 3, 3, 4, 4, 4, 4, 4, 4) will be made in the neckband later on, so the spacing of the buttonholes needs to take that into account.

Make each buttonhole as follows: BO 2 sts and, on the next row, CO 2 new sts over the gap.

After 6th row of ribbing, BO in ribbing.

Make another buttonhole band the same way on the other side of front.

Now work ribbing on neck. With color A and smaller-size needle, pick up and knit 5 sts at end of 1 buttonhole band, knit held sts, pick up and knit sts on end of next buttonhole band. Work 6 rows in k1, p1 ribbing, and, on the 2nd row, make a buttonhole at each side as follows:

3 sts ribbing, BO 2 sts, work in ribbing until 5 sts rem, BO 2 sts, rib 3. On next row, CO 2 sts over each gap.

BACK (WITH SLEEVE STITCHES)
The 1st row = WS. Work back and forth in stripe pattern.

On each RS row, decrease at raglan markers as before, and at each end, as for front shaping.

When you've decreased a total of 15 (15, 16, 17, 18, 19, 21, 25, 27, 29, 31) times for the raglan shaping, place sts on a holder.

Make bands as on front, omitting buttonholes. Finally, make ribbing on neck as for front without buttonholes.

FINISHING
Seam underarms. Sew down lower edges of button bands on yoke and sew on buttons. Weave in all ends neatly on WS.
Place damp towel on sweater and leave until completely dry.

Begin raglan shaping:
Decrease rnd: *K2, sl 1, k1, psso, *knit until 4 sts before marker, k2tog, k2*; rep * to * around = 8 sts decreased.

Decrease the same way on every other rnd. There should be 4 sts between the decreases at each raglan marker. On the 4th rnd of raglan decreasing, BO the 4 sts at raglan markers on front and work front separately from this point.

Place and back and sleeve sts on holder.

FRONT IN STRIPE PATTERN:
Row 1 (WS): Purl.
Row 2 (RS): Shape as follows: Sl 1, k1, psso, knit until 2 sts rem, k2tog.
Rep Rows 1–2 until you've decreased 11 (11, 12, 13, 14, 15, 17, 21 23, 25, 27) times = total of 15 (15, 16, 17, 18, 19, 21, 25, 27, 29, 31) times, including increases before you divided front and back.

Placed front sts on a holder.

Golden Headband: color 1042
Little Crafty Cap: color 1042
Winter Fine Vest: color 7251
Winter Fine Overalls: color 2652
Party Outfit Socks: color 1013
Block-Pattern Shorts: color 1055
Albert Mittens: color 7251

Preschool and School Clothes

Play Pants

Easy pants that can be worn for almost all activities and that are always good to have on hand. They are nice for nursery school and, in wool, under a ski or sledding outfit. This version is knitted in one color but it can easily be striped or patterned using stash yarn.

Level 2

SIZES: 1 (2, 4, 6, 8, 10) years

FINISHED MEASUREMENTS
Waist: Approx. 19¾ (21, 22½, 23¾, 25¼, 27¼) in [50 (53, 57, 60, 64, 69) cm]
Total Length: Approx. 14¼ (17¼, 22¾, 26¾, 29½, 33) in [36 (44, 58, 68, 75, 84) cm]

MATERIALS
YARN: Sandnes Garn KlompeLompe Merinoull (Merino wool) [CYCA #3 – DK, light worsted, 100% Merino superwash wool, 114 yd (104 m) / 50 g]
YARN COLORS AND AMOUNTS:
Color 6571: 150 (200, 200, 250, 300, 400) g
NEEDLES: US sizes 2.5 and 4 (3 and 3.5 mm): 24 and 32 in (60 and 80 cm) circulars and sets of 5 dpn; or use 32 in (80 cm) circular for magic loop (see video on magic loop technique on klompelompe.no).
NOTIONS: Waistband to fit waist + seam allowance

GAUGE: 22 sts on larger-size needles = 4 in (10 cm).
Adjust needle size to obtain correct gauge if necessary.

The pants are worked top down and knitted in the round.

With smaller-size circular, CO 112 (120, 128, 136, 144, 156) sts. Join, being careful not to twist cast-on row; pm for beginning of rnd. Knit 9 rnds, purl 1 rnd, knit 4 rnds.

Next rnd (eyelets for tie cords): k49 (53, 57, 61, 65, 71), k2tog, yo, k10, yo, sl 1, k1, psso, k49 (53, 57, 61, 65, 71). Knit 5 rnds. Change to larger-size circular and knit 1 rnd.

Now work short rows to raise the back. K10; turn, yo, p20; turn, yo, knit until 4 sts past previous turn (when you come to a yarnover, knit/purl it together with following st); turn, yo and purl until 4 sts past previous turn. Continue the same way until you've turned 4 (5, 5, 6, 6, 7) times on each side. Continue in stockinette. Knit 1 rnd, joining yarnovers with following st as you come to them.

Knit until piece measures 4 (4¾, 5½, 6¼, 7, 7½) in [10 (12, 14, 16, 18, 19) cm] after row where you changed to larger-size needle. Pm at each side of 10 sts at center front and center back.

Increase 1 st with M1 before and after each group of 10 marked sts at front and back = 4 sts increased on rnd.
    Increase the same way every 1¼ in (3 cm) a total of 5 times = 132 (140,148, 156, 164, 176) sts. On the next rnd, BO the 10 marked st at front and back = 56 (60, 64, 68, 72, 78) sts rem for each leg.

Work each leg separately. The legs are worked in the round. Change to dpn when sts no longer fit around circular.
    The 1st st of the rnd is always purled = marked st.

Work in stockinette for 1¼ in (3 cm). Decrease 1 st before and after marked st. Decrease the same way every 1¼ in (3 cm) a total of 5 (5, 6, 6, 7, 7) times. Continue in stockinette until pants measure 13 (16¼, 21¾, 25½, 28¼, 32) in [33 (41, 55, 65, 72, 81) cm] from round where you changed to larger-size needle.

Next rnd: Decrease 6 (6, 8, 8, 6, 8) sts evenly spaced around = 40 (44, 44, 48, 52, 56) sts rem.

Change to smaller-size dpn. Work around in k2, p2 ribbing for 1¼ in (3 cm). BO in ribbing.
    Work the other leg the same way.

FINISHING

Seam the 10 sts each of front and back crotch with mattress st. Fold waistband. Seam and insert waistband elastic in casing, then sew down casing on WS.

Make a 3-st I-cord (see I-cord on page 127) about 26 (26¾, 27½, 28¼, 29½, 30¼) in [66 (68, 70, 72, 75, 77) cm] long. If you have one, use a knitting mill to knit I-cord.

Weave in all ends neatly on WS.
Lay damp towel on pants and leave until completely dry.

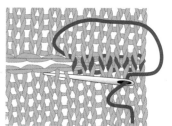

Mattress stitch

Easter Pullover:
color 4321,
Golden Headband:
Colors 4032 and
1042

Golden Cap

A totally stylish autumn cap that fits well. The pattern ribbing is easy to knit but it yields an impressive result. You can vary the look by adding a tassel, a crocheted flower, or wooden buttons.

SIZES: Newborn (0–2, 3–6, 9–12 months, 1–2, 3–6, 8–12 years)

MATERIALS

YARN: Sandnes Garn KlompeLompe Merinoull (Merino wool) [CYCA #3 – DK, light worsted, 100% Merino superwash wool, 114 yd (104 m) / 50 g]

YARN COLORS AND AMOUNTS:
Color 1042: 50 (50, 50, 50, 50, 50, 100) g

NEEDLES: US size 4 (3.5 mm): 16 in (40 cm) circular and set of 5 dpn

GAUGE: 22 sts = 4 in (10 cm).
Adjust needle size to obtain correct gauge if necessary.

The cap is knitted in the round on a circular needle.

CO 64 (68, 72, 76, 80, 88, 88) sts. Join, being careful not to twist cast-on row; pm for beginning of rnd.
    Work around in pattern ribbing:
    Rnds 1 and 2: *K1tbl, p1*; rep * to * around.
    Rnd 3: *Yo, k1tbl, p1, k1tbl, pass yo over the 3 sts, p1*; rep * to * around.

Rep ribbing pattern a total of 8 (10, 12, 13, 15, 16, 17) times.

Crown Shaping (move sts to dpn when they no longer fit around circular)
    Decrease Rnd 1: *Sl 1, k2tog, psso, p1, k1tbl, p1, k1tbl, p1*; rep * to * until 0 (4, 0, 4, 0, 0, 0) sts rem. If 4 sts rem, sl 1, k2tog, psso, p1.
    Next rnd: *K1tbl, p1*; rep * to * around.

Pattern rnd: *K1tbl, p1, yo, k1tbl, p1, k1tbl, pass yo over, p1* rep * to * until 0 (2, 0, 2, 0, 0, 0) sts rem. If 2 sts rem, k1 tbl, p1.
    Next 2 rnds: *K1tbl, p1*; rep * to * around.

Decrease Rnd 2: *K1 tbl, p1, sl 1, k2tog, psso, p1*; rep * to * until 0 (2, 0, 2, 0, 0, 0) sts rem. If 2 sts rem, k1 tbl, p1.
    Next 3 rnds: *K1tbl, p1*; rep * to * around.

Decrease Rnd 3: *Sl 1, k2tog, psso, p1*; rep * to * until 0 (2, 0, 2, 0, 0, 0) sts rem. If 2 sts rem, k1 tbl, p1.
Next rnd: *K1tbl, p1*; rep * to * around.

Decrease Rnd 4: *Sl 1, k2tog, psso, p1*; rep * to * until 0 (2, 0, 2, 0, 0, 0) sts rem. If 2 sts rem, k1, p1.

Cut yarn and draw end through rem sts; tighten.

Earflaps (for the smallest sizes, newborn to 1–2 years): There should be 10 (12, 14, 16, 16) sts between the flaps at center back With RS facing, pick up and knit 14 (16, 18, 18, 20) sts.
    Purl 1 row, knit 1 row, purl 1 row.
    Shape earflap as follows:
    Every RS Row: K1, sl 1, k1, psso, knit until 3 sts rem, k2tog, k1.
Every WS Row: Purl.
Rep these 2 rows until 4 sts rem.
Next RS Row: K1, k2tog, k1.
Now make an I-cord 8 in (20 cm) long—see below.
Make 2nd earflap the same way.

FINISHING

Weave in all ends neatly on WS.
Lay damp towel on cap and leave until completely dry.

I-CORD
CO 3 (4) sts on dpn. Knit all rows.
K3, *slide sts back to front needle tip.
Bring yarn across WS. K3, tightening
yarn a bit with first st. Rep from * until
cord is desired length.
(See video on klompelompe.no.)

Golden Headband

A texture you can go crazy over. The headband is quick to knit and perfect as a gift. It can easily be paired with, for example, the Golden Mittens.

SIZES: 6–9 months (1–2, 3–6, 7–10, 10–14 years)

MATERIALS
YARN: Sandnes Garn KlompeLompe Merinoull (Merino wool) [CYCA #3 – DK, light worsted, 100% Merino superwash wool, 114 yd (104 m) / 50 g]
YARN COLORS AND AMOUNTS:
Color 4032: 50 (50, 50, 50, 50) g
NEEDLES: US size 4 (3.5 mm): 16 in (40 cm) circular

GAUGE: 22 sts = 4 in (10 cm).
Adjust needle size to obtain correct gauge if necessary.

CO 76 (80, 84, 88, 92) sts. Join, being careful not to twist cast-on row; pm for beginning of rnd.

Work around in pattern ribbing:
    Rnds 1 and 2: *K1tbl, p1*; rep * to * around.
    Rnd 3: *Yo, k1tbl, p1, k1tbl, pass yo over the 3 sts, p1*; rep * to * around.

Rep ribbing pattern a total of 7 (8, 9, 10, 11) times, work rnds 1–2, binding off in pattern on Rnd 2.

FINISHING
Weave in all ends neatly on WS.
Lay damp towel on headband and leave until completely dry.

Golden Mittens

Mittens to match the Golden Cap. Make them in the smallest size for a perfect christening gift.

→→

SIZES: 0–2 months (3–6, 9 months, 1–2, 3–6, 8–10,12–14 years)

MATERIALS

YARN: Sandnes Garn KlompeLompe Merinoull (Merino wool) [CYCA #3 – DK, light worsted, 100% Merino superwash wool, 114 yd (104 m) / 50 g]

YARN COLORS AND AMOUNTS:
Color 4032: 50 (50, 50, 50, 100, 100, 100) g
NEEDLES: US size 4 (3.5 mm): Set of 5 dpn or 32 in (80 cm) circular for magic loop (see video at klopelompe.no)

GAUGE: 22 sts = 4 in (10 cm).
Adjust needle size to obtain correct gauge if necessary.

CO 28 (32, 32, 36, 36, 40, 40) sts. Divide st onto dpn and join.

Work around in pattern ribbing:
Rnds 1 and 2: *K1tbl, p1*; rep * to * around.
Rnd 3: *Yo, k1tbl, p1, k1tbl, pass yo over the 3 sts, p1*; rep * to * around.

Rep ribbing pattern a total of 3 (4, 4, 5, 5, 6, 6) times. Work Rnd 1.

On next rnd, make eyelets for ties:

0–2 months:
Yo, k2, k2tog, yo, k5, k2tog, yo, k2, k2tog, yo, k2, k2tog, yo, k3, k2tog, yo, k2, k2tog.

3–6 and 9 months:
Yo, k1, k2tog, yo, k1, k2tog, yo, k3, k2tog, yo, *k1, k2tog, yo*; rep * to * a total of 6 times, ending with k1, k2tog.

1–2 and 3–6 years:
Yo, k1, k2tog, yo, k1, k2tog, yo, k7, k2tog, yo, *k1, k2tog, yo*; rep * to * a total of 6 times, ending with k1, k2tog.

8–10 and 12–14 years:
K2, k2tog, yo; rep * to * around.

Next rnd:
Pm, k1tbl, p1, k1tbl, pm, k11 (13, 13, 15, 15, 17,17), pm, k1tbl, p1, k1tbl, pm, k11 (13, 13, 15, 15, 17, 17).

On the 3 sts at each side, work in pattern as follows:
Rnd 1: Yo, k1tbl, p1, k1tbl, pass yo over the 3 sts.
Rnds 2–3: K1tbl p1, k1tbl.

Work rem sts on rnd in stockinette (knit every rnd).

Thumb for sizes 1–2, 3–6, 8–10, and 12–14 years:
When mitten measures 3¼ (3½, 4½, 4½) in [8 (9, 11.5, 11.5) cm], set up thumbhole as follows:

Right Mitten: Work 3 sts in pattern, knit 6 sts with smooth, contrast color waste yarn; slide 6 sts back to left needle and knit them again with mitten yarn. Continue to end of rnd as est.

Left Mitten: Work 3 sts in pattern, k8 (8, 11, 11), knit 6 sts with smooth, contrast color waste yarn; slide 6 sts back to left needle and knit them again with mitten yarn. Continue as est.

When mitten measures 3½ (4¼, 4¾, 5½, 6¼, 7¼, 8) in [9 (11, 12, 14, 16, 18.5, 20) cm], shape top over the stockinette sections, between the ribbed bands:
Sl 1, k1, psso, knit until 2 sts before marker, k2tog.
Decrease the same way on every other rnd, 3 times and then on every rnd until 3 stockinette sts rem on each side of mitten.
Next rnd: With rem 3 knit sts: sl 1, k2tog, psso.
Cut yarn, draw end through rem sts; tighten.

THUMB
Insert a dpn into 6 sts below waste yarn and another dpn into 6 sts above waste yarn. Carefully remove waste yarn. Divide sts onto 3 dpn and knit around for 1½ (2, 2½, 2¾) in [4 (5, 6, 7) cm].
K2tog around; cut yarn, draw end through rem sts; tighten.

FINISHING
Weave in all ends neatly on WS.
Twist a tie cord about 15¾ in (40 cm) long for each mitten, preferably in a contrasting color. Lay damp towel on mittens and leave until completely dry.

On Tora: Heritage Pullover: color A 2652, color B 1013, color C 4032. Golden Cap: color 4344.
On Henry: Autumn Cap: color 101

Heritage Pullover

A pullover with a classic round yoke and a fun stranded colorwork pattern for both girls and boys. It is good and warm, and we decided to knit it in a lovely Merino wool yarn so it won't prickle and will keep its shape well. Maybe little brother will inherit one from big sister?

SIZES: 1 (2, 4, 6, 8, 10, 12 years)

FINISHED MEASUREMENTS

Chest: Approx. 24½ (25¼, 26½, 29¼, 32¼, 35, 36¼) in [62 (64.5, 67, 74.5, 82, 89, 92) cm]

Total Length: Approx. 13¾ (15¾, 18¼, 19, 19¾, 21¼, 22) in [35 (40, 46, 48, 50, 54, 56) cm]

MATERIALS

YARN: Sandnes Garn KlompeLompe Merinoull (fine Merino wool) [CYCA #3 – DK, light worsted, 100% Merino superwash wool, 114 yd (104 m) / 50 g]

YARN COLORS AND AMOUNTS:

Color A 1020: 50 (50, 50, 50, 50, 50, 50) g
Color B 1013: 50 (50, 50, 50, 50, 50, 50) g
Color C 6061: 200 (200, 250, 300, 350, 400, 400) g

NEEDLES: US size 2.5 and 6 (3 and 4 mm): 16 and 24 in (40 and 60 cm) circulars and sets of 5 dpn

GAUGE: 22 sts on larger-size needles = 4 in (10 cm).
Adjust needle size to obtain correct gauge if necessary.

The sweater is worked in the round on a circular needle, from top down.

With smaller-size circular and color A, CO 72 (76, 80, 84, 84, 84, 88) sts. Join, being careful not to twist cast-on row; pm for beginning of rnd.

Work around in k1, p1 ribbing for 2 in (5 cm).
Change to larger-size circular. Knit 1 rnd, increasing 28 (30, 34, 42, 46, 54, 54) sts evenly spaced around = 100 (106, 114, 126, 130, 138, 142) sts.

Now work following chart. Make sure that the floats are not too tight and pull in. If necessary, use a larger-size needle for stranded colorwork.
After completing charted rows, 180 (192,

204, 216, 216, 228, 240) sts rem. Knit 1 rnd with color C. On the next rnd, increase 40 (40, 42, 36, 36, 45, 45) sts evenly spaced around = 220 (232, 246, 252, 252, 273, 285) sts. Knit 3 rnds. On the next rnd, increase 0 (0, 0, 18, 42, 45, 47) sts evenly spaced around = 220 (232, 246, 270, 294, 318, 332) sts.

Now divide body and sleeves: Place 50 (54, 58, 62, 66, 70, 74) sts on a holder for 1 sleeve; CO 9 sts for underarm, k60 (62, 65, 73, 81, 89, 92); place 50 (54, 58, 62, 66, 70, 74) sts on a holder for 1 sleeve; CO 9 sts for underarm; k60 (62, 65, 73, 81, 89, 92) = 138 (142, 148, 164, 180, 196, 202) sts rem for body.

Sizes 1 (2, 4) years

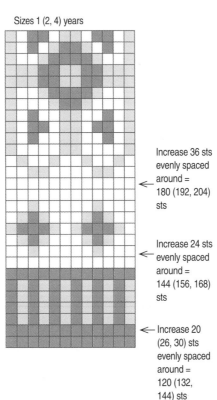

← Increase 36 sts evenly spaced around = 180 (192, 204) sts

← Increase 24 sts evenly spaced around = 144 (156, 168) sts

← Increase 20 (26, 30) sts evenly spaced around = 120 (132, 144) sts

Sizes 6 (8, 10, 12) years

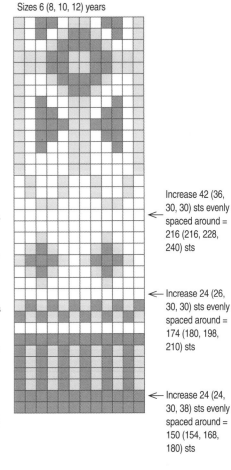

← Increase 42 (36, 30, 30) sts evenly spaced around = 216 (216, 228, 240) sts

← Increase 24 (26, 30, 30) sts evenly spaced around = 174 (180, 198, 210) sts

← Increase 24 (24, 30, 38) sts evenly spaced around = 150 (154, 168, 180) sts

■ Color A
▨ Color B
□ Color C (MC)

Work around in stockinette (knit all rnds) until body measures 6½ (7¾, 9½, 10¼, 11½ , 12¼, 13½) in [16.5 (19.5, 24.5, 26, 29, 31, 34) cm] below underarm.
Change to smaller-size circular and work around in k1, p1 ribbing for 1½ in (4 cm). BO in ribbing.

SLEEVES

With larger-size dpn (or magic loop circular) and color C, CO 4 sts, knit 50 (54, 58, 62, 66, 70, 74) held sleeve sts, CO 5 sts; pm for beginning of rnd. Divide sts onto needle(s) and join.

Magic loop: See video on technique at klompelompe.no.

Knit around for ¾ in (2 cm). Now begin shaping sleeve as follows: K1, k2tog, knit until 3 sts rem, sl 1, k1, psso, k1.
Decrease the same way every 1¼ (1¼, 1¼, 1¼, 1¼, 1, 1) in [3 (3, 3, 3, 3, 2.5, 2.5) cm] until 47 (49, 51, 53, 55, 55, 55) sts rem. Continue in stockinette until sleeve is 7¼ (8½, 9½, 11, 12¼, 13, 14½) in [18.5 (21.5, 24.5, 28, 31, 33, 37) cm] long.
On the next rnd, decrease 7 sts evenly spaced around.

Change to smaller-size needle and work around in k1, p1 ribbing for 1⅜ (1⅜, 1½, 1½, 1½, 1, 1½) in [3.5 (3.5, 4, 4, 4, 4, 4) cm]. BO in ribbing.

Make the 2nd sleeve the same way.

FINISHING
Seam underarms.
Weave in all ends neatly on WS.
Place damp towel on sweater and leave until completely dry.

Ridged Mittens

Delightful garter stitch mittens. Pair the mittens with, for example, Pilot Cap's Little Brother, and you'll have a fine set for fall and winter.

SIZES: 1–2 (3–5, 6–8) years

MATERIALS

YARN: Sandnes Garn KlompeLompe Spøt [CYCA #3 – DK, light worsted, 40% Merino wool, 40% alpaca, 20% nylon, 147 yd (134 m) / 50 g]

YARN COLORS AND AMOUNTS:
Color 4321: 100 (100, 100) g

NEEDLES: US sizes 6 and 8 (4 and 5 mm): sets of 5 dpn or use 32 in (80 cm) circular for magic loop (see video on magic loop technique on klompelompe.no).

GAUGE: 18 sts on larger-size needles with 2 strands of yarn held together = 4 in (10 cm). Adjust needle size to obtain correct gauge if necessary.

The mittens are worked in the round on dpn or a long magic loop circular (for magic loop, see video at klompelompe.no).

With larger-size needles and holding 2 strands of yarn together, CO 28 (30, 32) sts. Divide sts onto dpn and join.

Work around in ridges: *knit 2 rnds, purl 2 rnds*; rep * to * for 3 (4, 5) ridges.

Knit 1 rnd.
Change to smaller-size dpn.
Work 7 (9, 9) rnds in k1, p1 ribbing.
Change to larger-size dpn.
Pm on each side (or divide sts onto dpn): 14 (15, 16) sts for front and 14 (15, 16) sts for back).

Work in ridges.

When mitten measures 1¼ (1½, 2¼) in [3 (4, 5.5) cm] from ribbing and you are on a knit round, place thumbhole:

Right mitten: Work across back, k1, knit 4 sts with smooth, contrast color waste yarn, slip the 4 sts back to left needle and knit with working yarn; knit rem 9 (10, 11) sts.

Left mitten: Work across back, k9 (10, 11), knit 4 sts with smooth, contrast color waste yarn, slip the 4 sts back to left needle and knit with working yarn; knit rem sts.

When mitten is approx. 3½ (4¼, 4¾) in [9 (11, 12) cm] above ribbing, and you've just worked a purl ridge, shape top as follows:

Front: K1, sl 1, k1, psso, knit until 3 sts rem on front, k2tog, k1. Rep on back the same way.
Continue in stockinette (knit all rnds).

Decrease the same way on every other rnd, 2 times and then on every rnd 2 (3) times.
Cut yarn, draw end through rem sts; tighten.

THUMB

Insert a dpn into 5 sts below waste yarn and another dpn into 5 sts above waste yarn. Carefully remove waste yarn. Divide sts onto 3 dpn and knit around for 1½ (2, 2½) in [4 (5, 6) cm].

K2tog around; cut yarn, draw end through rem sts; tighten.

FINISHING

Weave in all ends neatly on WS.
If necessary, stitch around any holes at sides of thumb and close openings.
Lay damp towel on mittens and leave until completely dry.

Color 4331 ⟶⟶

Tora Cap

One of our most popular patterns is the Tora headband from the first KlompeLompe book. We've now designed a cap constructed in the same style, and we think it's just as sweet as the headband.

SIZES: 6–24 months (3–6, 8–12 years)

MATERIALS
YARN: Sandnes Garn KlompeLompe Merinoull (Merino wool) [CYCA #3 – DK, light worsted, 100% Merino superwash wool, 114 yd (104 m) / 50 g]
YARN COLORS AND AMOUNTS:
Color 4032: 50 (50, 100) g + small amount of contrast color for I-cord
NEEDLES: US size 6 (4 mm): 16 in (40 cm) circular and set of 5 dpn

GAUGE: 22 sts = 4 in (10 cm).
Adjust needle size to obtain correct gauge if necessary.

The cap is knitted in the round on a circular needle.

Lace and Ribbing Pattern (multiple of 14 sts)
Rnd 1: *P1, k1, p1, k1, p1, k9*; rep * to * around.
Rnd 2: *P1, k1, p1, k1, p1, k2tog, k2, yo, k1, yo, k2, sl 1, p1, psso*; rep * to * around.

CO 70 (84, 84) sts. Join and pm at beginning of rnd.
Work lace and ribbing pattern 7 (9, 9) times.
    Knit 1 rnd, increasing 10 (4, 4) sts evenly spaced around = 80 (88, 88) sts.

Now work around in stockinette until cap measures 5½ (6¼, 7) in [14 (16, 18) cm].
    On next rnd, decrease 0 (8, 8) sts evenly spaced around = 80 (80, 80) sts rem.

Crown Shaping (move sts to dpn when thy no longer fit around circular)
    Decrease Rnd 1: *K6, k2tog*; rep * to * around.
    Knit 2 rnds.
Decrease Rnd 2: *K5, k2tog*; rep * to * around.
    Knit 2 rnds.

Decrease Rnd 3: *K4, k2tog*; rep * to * around.
    Knit 2 rnds.
Decrease Rnd 4: *K3, k2tog*; rep * to * around.
    Decrease Rnd 5: *K6, k2tog*; rep * to * around.
Decrease Rnd 6: *K5, k2tog*; rep * to * around.
    Decrease Rnd 7: *K4, k2tog*; rep * to * around.
    Decrease Rnd 8: *K3, k2tog*; rep * to * around.
Decrease Rnd 9: *K2, k2tog*; rep * to * around.
Decrease Rnd 10: *K2tog*; rep * to * around, ending with k1.

Cut yarn and draw end through rem sts; tighten.

FINISHING
Weave in all ends neatly on WS.
Make an I-cord about 33½ in (85 cm) long. See page 127 for I-cord instructions or use a knitting mill.
Lay damp towel on cap and leave until completely dry. Thread I-cord through lace (see photo).

Autumn Cap

A warm cap, excellent for autumn. This one is knitted with the cozy and pretty Du Store Alpakka Alpakka Tweed yarn.

Cap: Color 101

SIZES: 6–9 months (1–2, 3–6, 8–14 years, adult women)

MATERIALS

YARN: Du Store Alpakka Alpakka Tweed [CYCA #4 – Worsted, Afghan, Aran, 50% alpaca, 30% Merino wool, 20% Donegal fiber, 87 yd (80 m) / 50 g]

YARN COLORS AND AMOUNTS: Color 102: 50 (50, 100, 100, 100) g

NEEDLES: US size 8 (5 mm): 16 in (40 cm) circular and set of 5 dpn

NOTIONS: 2 decorative buttons (optional)

GAUGE: 17 sts = 4 in (10 cm). Adjust needle size to obtain correct gauge if necessary.

The cap is knitted in the round on a circular needle.

CO 58 (64, 64, 68, 68) sts. Join and pm at beginning of rnd.
Work 10 rnds k1, p1 ribbing.
Knit 1 rnd.
Knit 1 rnd, increasing 6 (8, 8, 12, 12) sts evenly spaced around = 64 (72, 72, 80, 80) sts.
Knit 3 (4, 5, 5, 6) rnds.
Now work in pattern.

ABBREVIATIONS

Wyf: with yarn in front of work
Wyb: with yarn in back of work
LLS: lift loose strand in front of work and knit it together with st.

PATTERN

Rnd 1: *P1, sl 3 wyf*; rep * to * around.
Rnds 2–3: Knit.
Rnd 4: K2, LLS, *k3, p1, LLS*; rep * to * until 1 st rem, k1.
Rnd 5: Sl 2 wyf, p1 *sl 3 wyf, p1*; rep * to * around until 1 st rem, sl 1 wyb.
Rnds 6–7: Knit.
Rnd 8: LLS, *k3, LLS*; rep * to * around until 3 sts rem, k3.

After working pattern sequence 2 (2.5, 3, 4, 5) times, continue in stockinette:
Knit 3 (3, 5, 7, 11) rnds.
Now shape crown.

Crown Shaping (move sts to dpn when thy no longer fit around circular)
Decrease Rnd 1: *K6, k2tog*; rep * to * around.
Knit 2 rnds.
Decrease Rnd 2: *K5, k2tog*; rep * to * around.
Knit 2 rnds.
Decrease Rnd 3: *K4, k2tog*; rep * to *

around.
Knit 1 rnd.
Decrease Rnd 4: *K3, k2tog*; rep * to * around.
Knit 1 rnd.
Decrease Rnd 5: *K2, k2tog*; rep * to * around.
Knit 1 rnd.
Decrease Rnd 6: *K1, k2tog*; rep * to * around.
Decrease Rnd 7: *K2tog*; rep * to * around.

Cut yarn and draw end through rem sts; tighten.

FINISHING

Weave in all ends neatly on WS.
Lay damp towel on cap and leave until completely dry. Sew on 2 decorative buttons if desired (see photos).

Fall

Chunky Pullover for Children

A feather-light cozy sweater knitted with the softest silk and mohair yarn.
The pullover is oversized and snuggly but also fits well with raglan shaping and
a split back. Ribbing around the neck and sleeve cuffs worked with a single
fine yarn gives the garment a delicate finish.

SIZES: 1 (2, 4, 6, 8, 10, 12 years)

FINISHED MEASUREMENTS
Chest: Approx. 22 (23¼, 25, 27¾, 30, 31½, 33½) in [56 (59, 63.5, 70.5, 76.5, 80, 85) cm]
Total Length: Approx. 11½ (13, 15, 16¼, 17¾, 19¼, 20) in [29 (33, 38, 41, 45, 49, 51) cm]

MATERIALS
YARN: Sandnes Garn Alpakka Silke [CYCA #1 – fingering, 70% alpaca, 30% mulberry silk, 219 yd (200 m) / 50 g]
Sandnes Garn Silk Mohair [CYCA #0 – lace, 60% mohair, 25% silk, 15% wool, 306 yd (280 m) / 50 g]
YARN COLORS AND AMOUNTS:
Alpakka Silke: Color 6041: 100 (100, 150, 150, 200, 200, 200) g

Silk Mohair: Color 1076: 50 (50, 100, 100, 100, 100, 100) g
NEEDLES: US size 8 (5 mm): 24 in (60 cm) circular and set of 5 dpn
US size 2.5 (3 mm): 16 in (40 cm) circular and set of 5 dpn
Or 32 in (80 cm) circulars for magic loop technique (for magic loop, see video at klompelompe. no)

GAUGE: 17 sts on larger-size needles with 1 strand of each yarn held together = 4 in (10 cm).
27 sts on smaller size needles with single strand of Alpakka Silke = 4 in (10 cm).
Adjust needle size to obtain correct gauge if necessary.

The sweater is worked bottom up, beginning back and forth in garter stitch with two strands of yarn held together.

BACK
Begin with right back.
    With larger-size circular and holding 1 strand of each yarn together, CO 26 (28, 31, 35, 37, 40, 43) sts.
    Knit 7 ridges (= knit 14 rows). Set piece aside.

Make left back as for right back. Set piece aside.

FRONT
With larger size circular and holding 1 strand of each yarn together, CO 52 (56, 62, 70, 74, 80, 86) sts. Knit 4 ridges (= knit 8 rows).

Join all pieces onto same circular.

Begin with left back, then front, and right back = 104 (112, 124, 140, 148, 160, 172) sts total. Pm at each side (between right back and front, and left back and front).
    Work back and forth.

Take all measurements from beginning of row = center back.

When body measures 2¾ (2¾, 3¼, 3¼, 4, 4, 4) in [7 (7, 8, 8, 10, 10, 10) cm], decrease at each marker (on RS) as follows:
    Knit until 3 sts before marker, k2tog, k2, k2tog. Rep decreases the same way at next marker. You've now decreased 1 st on each side of each marker = 4 sts decreased.

Rep the decrease row every 1¼ in (3 cm), always on a RS row until 96 (100, 108, 120, 128, 136, 144) sts rem.

Continue without further shaping until body measures 5½ (6¾, 8¼, 9½, 10¾, 11¾, 12¾) in [14 (17, 21, 24, 27, 30, 32) cm] and you have just knitted a WS row.
    Cut yarn. Move sts from left back to right needle and begin rnd on left side from now on. Pm for beginning of rnd.

    Now join and begin garter st in the round (= knit 1 rnd, purl 1 rnd). Work around for 2 in (5 cm). Body now measures 7½ (8¾, 10¼, 11½, 12¾, 13¾, 14½) in [19 (22, 26, 29, 32, 35, 37) cm] long at center back.

On the next rnd (knit), shape armholes as follows:

BO 4 sts, k40 (42, 46, 52, 56, 60, 64), BO 8 sts, k40 (42, 46, 52, 56, 60, 64), BO 4 sts.

Set body aside while you knit sleeves.

SLEEVES

With smaller-size dpn and single strand of Alpakka Silke, CO 40 (44, 44, 44, 48, 48, 48) sts. Divide sts onto dpn and join.

Work around in k2, p2 ribbing for 1½ (1½, 1¾, 1¾, 2, 2, 2) in [4 (4, 4.5, 4.5, 5, 5, 5) cm]. Pm at beginning of rnd = center of underarm.

Change to larger-size dpn and work with 1 strand each of Alpakka Silke and Silk Mohair.

Knit 1 rnd, decreasing 10 (12, 12, 12, 14, 14, 14) sts evenly spaced around = 30 (32, 32, 32, 34, 34, 34) sts rem.

Continue in garter st in the round (= purl 1 rnd, knit 1 rnd).

When sleeve measures 2¾ (2¾, 3¼, 3¼, 4, 4, 4) in [7 (7, 8, 8, 10, 10, 10) cm] and the next rnd is a knit rnd, increase 1 st at each side of marker as follows:

Increase rnd: K1, M1, knit until 1 st before marker M1, k1.

Rep the increase rnd every 1¼ (1¼, 1⅜, 1⅜, 1⅝, 1⅜, 1⅝) in [3 (3, 3.5, 3.5, 4, 3.5, 4) cm until there are 38 (42, 42, 44, 46, 48, 48) sts.

Continue in garter st until sleeve is approx. 8¼ (9¾, 10¾, 12¼, 13½, 14½, 15¾) in

[21 (25, 27, 31, 34, 37, 40) cm] long and you have just purled a rnd.

On the next rnd, BO 8 sts centered on underarm.

Set sleeve aside while you knit 2nd sleeve the same way.

JOIN BODY AND SLEEVES

Arrange body and sleeves on larger-size circular = 140 (152, 160, 176, 188, 200, 208) sts. Pm at each intersection of body and sleeve = 4 markers.

Rnd begins before left sleeve; pm.

Work 3 rnds in garter st (purl 1 rnd, knit 1 rnd, purl 1 rnd).

On the next rnd (knit), decrease at the markers as follows:

Raglan decrease rnd: *K2tog, knit until 2 sts before next marker, k2tog tbl*; rep * to * around = 8 sts decreased.

Continue in garter st ridges, decreasing on every other rnd (on the knit rnds) a total of 10 (11, 12, 13, 15, 16, 16) times until 60 (64, 64, 72, 68, 72, 80) sts rem.

Change to smaller-size circular and a single strand of Alpakka Silke. Knit 1 rnd, increasing 32 (32, 36, 32, 40, 40, 36) sts evenly spaced around = 92 (96, 100, 104, 108, 112, 116) sts.

Work around in k2, p2 ribbing for 1¼ in (3 cm). On the last rnd, BO loosely in ribbing (we recommend using a larger-size needle),

FINISHING

With RS facing, smaller-size circular and a single strand of Alpakka Silke, pick up and knit about 1 st for every row along 1 side of split back. Work back and forth in stockinette for 3½ in (9 cm), ending with a WS row, join to opposite side of split with Kitchener st (see photos below). If that is a bit difficult, BO and then join with mattress st (see page 124).

Sew a tuck at the top of the split.

Weave in all ends neatly on WS.
Lay damp towel on sweater and leave until completely dry.

Chunky Pullover for Adults

SIZES: XS (S–M, L–XL)

FINISHED MEASUREMENTS
Chest: Approx. 35 (37, 40¾) in [89 (94, 103.5) cm]
Total Length: Approx. 21¾ (23¾, 26) in [55 (60, 66) cm]

MATERIALS
YARN: Sandnes Garn Alpakka Silke [CYCA #1 – fingering, 70% alpaca, 30% mulberry silk, 219 yd (200 m) / 50 g]
Sandnes Garn Silk Mohair [CYCA #0 – lace, 60% mohair, 25% silk, 15% wool, 306 yd (280 m) / 50 g]
YARN COLORS AND AMOUNTS:
Alpakka Silke: Color 7572: 200 (250, 300) g
Silk Mohair: Color 7572: 150 (150, 200) g
NEEDLES: US size 8 (5 mm): 24 in (60 cm) circular and set of 5 dpn
US size 2.5 (3 mm): 16 in (40 cm) circular and set of 5 dpn
Or 32 in (80 cm) circulars for magic loop technique (for magic loop, see video at klompelompe. no)

GAUGE: 17 sts on larger size needles with 1 strand of each yarn held together = 4 in (10 cm).
27 sts on smaller-size needles with single strand of Alpakka Silke = 4 in (10 cm).
Adjust needle size to obtain correct gauge if necessary.

The sweater is worked bottom up, beginning back and forth in garter stitch with 2 strands of yarn held together.

BACK
Begin with right back.
With larger-size circular and holding 1 strand of each yarn together, CO 45 (48, 53) sts.
Knit 10 ridges (= knit 20 rows). Set piece aside.

Make left back as for right back. Set piece aside.

FRONT
With larger-size circular and holding 1 strand of each yarn together, CO 90 (96, 106) sts. Knit 6 ridges (= knit 12 rows).

Join all pieces onto same circular.
Begin with left back, then front, and right back = 180 (192, 212) sts total. Pm at each side (between right back and front, and left back and front).
Work back and forth.

Take all measurements from beginning of row = center back.

When body measures 4¾ (4¾, 4¾) in [12 (12, 12) cm], decrease at each marker (on RS) as follows:
Knit until 3 sts before marker, k2tog, k2, k2tog. Rep decreases the same way at next marker. You've now decreased 1 st on each side of each marker = 4 sts decreased.

Rep the decrease row every 1¼ in (3 cm), always on a RS row until 152 (160, 176) sts rem.

Continue without further shaping until body measures 13 (14¼, 15½) in [33 (36, 39) cm] and you have just knitted a WS row.
Cut yarn. Move sts from left back to right needle and begin rnd on left side from now on. Pm for beginning of rnd.

Now join and begin garter st in the round (= knit 1 rnd, purl 1 rnd). Work around for 2¾ in (7 cm). Body now measures 15¾ (17, 18¼) in [40 (43, 46) cm] long at center back.

On the next rnd (knit), shape armholes as follows:
BO 4 sts, k68 (72, 80), BO 8 sts, k68 (72, 80), BO 4 sts.
Set body aside while you knit sleeves.

SLEEVES
With smaller-size dpn and single strand of Alpakka Silke, CO 52 (56, 60) sts. Divide sts onto dpn and join.
Work around in k2, p2 ribbing for 2½ (2½, 2½) in [6 (6, 6) cm]. Pm at beginning of rnd = center of underarm.
Change to larger-size dpn and work with 1 strand each of Alpakka Silke and Silk Mohair held together.
Knit 1 rnd, decreasing 16 (17, 19) sts evenly spaced around = 36 (39, 41) sts rem.
Continue in garter st in the round (= purl 1 rnd, knit 1 rnd).

When sleeve measures 4 (4, 4) in [10 (10, 10) cm] and the next rnd is a knit rnd, increase 1 st at each side of marker as follows:
Increase Rnd: K1, M1, knit until 1 st before marker M1, k1.
Rep the increase rnd every 2 (1¾, 1½) in [5 (4.5, 4) cm] until there are 50 (55, 59) sts.

146

Continue in garter st until sleeve is approx. 18½ (18½, 18½) in [47 (47, 47) cm] long and you have just purled a rnd.

On the next rnd, BO 8 sts centered on underarm.

Set sleeve aside while you knit 2nd sleeve the same way.

JOIN BODY AND SLEEVES

Arrange body and sleeves on larger-size circular = 220 (238, 262) sts. Pm at each intersection of body and sleeve = 4 markers.

Rnd begins before left sleeve; pm.

Work 11 rnds in garter st (purl 1 rnd, knit 1 rnd, etc.).

On the next rnd (knit), decrease at the markers as follows:

Raglan decrease rnd: *K2tog, knit until 2 sts before next marker, k2tog tbl*; rep * to * around = 8 sts decreased.

Continue in garter st ridges, decreasing on every other rnd (on the knit rnds) a total of 15 (17, 19) times until 100 (102, 110) sts rem.

Change to smaller-size circular and a single strand of Alpakka Silke. Knit 1 rnd, increasing 56 (54, 50) sts evenly spaced around = 156 (156, 160) sts.

Work around in k2, p2 ribbing for 1½ in (4 cm). On the last rnd, BO loosely in ribbing (we recommend using a larger-size needle),

FINISHING

With RS facing, smaller-size circular and a single strand of Alpakka Silke, pick up and knit about 1 st for every row along 1 side of split back. Work back and forth in stockinette for 3½ in (9 cm), ending with a WS row, join to opposite side of split with Kitchener st (see photos on page 145). If that is a bit difficult, BO and then join with mattress st (see page 124).

Sew a tuck at the top of the split.

Weave in all ends neatly on WS.
Lay damp towel on sweater and leave until completely dry.

Cozy Socks

When it gets dark earlier and the tealights are lit, it's time to curl up on the sofa. Your feet won't freeze for long while you wait for these socks, because they knit up quickly on size US 11 (7 mm) needles, even if you are a beginner knitter.

SIZES: 1 (2–4, 6–8, 10–14 years; women's)

MATERIALS
YARN: Sandnes Garn Smart [CYCA #3 – DK, light worsted, 100% superwash wool, 109 yd (100 m) / 50 g]
YARN COLORS AND AMOUNTS:
Color 1015: 100 (100, 150, 150, 200) g
NEEDLES: US size 11 (7 mm): magic loop or very short circular and set of 5 dpn

GAUGE: 14 sts with 2 strands of yarn held together = 4 in (10 cm).
Adjust needle size to obtain correct gauge if necessary.

With 2 strands of yarn held together, CO 20 (24, 28, 28, 32) sts. Join and pm for beginning of rnd. Work around in k1, p1 ribbing for 1¼, (1½, 1½, 2½, 2½) in [3 (4, 4, 6, 6) cm].

DOUBLE SEED STITCH
Rnds 1–2: *K2, p2*; rep * to * around.
Rnds 3–4: *P2, k2*; rep * to * around.
Rep Rnds 1–4 for pattern.

Work around in Double Seed st until sock measures 4¾ (6, 8¼, 9½, 9¾) in [12 (15, 21, 24, 25) cm].

Knit 1 rnd, decreasing 6 (6, 6, 0, 0) sts evenly spaced around = 14 (18, 22, 28, 32) sts rem.

Place the 1st and last 4 (5, 6, 7, 8) sts on a holder and work the rem 6 (8, 10, 14, 16) sts separately.

INSTEP (FRONT)
Work back and forth in stockinette over the 6 (8, 10, 14, 16) sts until instep measures 1½ (2½, 3¼, 4, 5¼) in [4 (6, 8, 10, 13) cm].
    Decrease row (RS): K2tog, knit until 2 sts rem, sl 1, k1, psso.
    Rep the decrease row on every RS row a total of 2 (2, 2, 3, 3) times.
    BO on next (WS) row.

Begin rnd where the rnd began previously. K4 (5, 6, 7, 8) from holder, pick up and knit sts around instep, 1 st in each st across, but at the sides, skip every 4th st; k4 (5, 6, 7, 8) from holder = 30 (36, 52, 58, 70) sts total. Work around in garter ridges (= alternate purl 1 rnd, knit 1 rnd). When you've worked 1.5 (1.5, 2.5, 3.5, 4.5) ridges and the next rnd is a knit rnd, decrease as follows:
    Decrease Rnd 1: K1, k2tog, k9 (11, 18, 20, 26), k2tog, k2 (4, 6, 8, 8), k2tog, k9 (11, 18, 20, 26), k2tog, k1.
    Purl 1 rnd.

Decrease Rnd 2: K1, k2tog, k7 (9, 16, 18, 24), k2tog, k2 (4, 6, 8, 8), k2tog, k7 (9, 16, 18, 24), k2tog, k1 = 22 (28, 44, 50, 62) sts rem.
    Purl 1 rnd.

Decrease Rnd 3: K1, k2tog, k4 (7, 15, 18, 24), k2tog, k1, k2tog, k1, k2tog, (4, 7, 15, 18, 24), k2tog, k1.
    Purl 1 rnd.
    Knit 1 rnd, binding off.

Make 2nd sock the same way.

FINISHING
Seam sole. Weave in all ends neatly on WS. Lay damp towel on socks and leave until completely dry.

Pilot Cap's Little Brother

The well-known pilot's cap in a new, simpler version.
A totally new construction but with the same good fit.

SIZES: 6–12 months (1–3, 3–6, 8–12 years)

MATERIALS
YARN: Sandnes Garn KlompeLompe
Merinoull (Merino wool) [CYCA #3 – DK, light
worsted, 100% Merino wool, 114 yd (104 m)
/ 50 g]
YARN COLORS AND AMOUNTS:
Color 2652: 50 (100, 100, 100) g
NEEDLES: US size 6 (4 mm): 16 in (40 cm)
circular and set of 5 dpn
CROCHET HOOK: US size G-6 (4 mm)
NOTIONS: 2 buttons

GAUGE: 22 sts = 4 in (10 cm).
Adjust needle size to obtain correct gauge
if necessary.

With circular, or dpn, CO 72 (80, 80, 88) sts.
Join and pm at beginning of rnd.

Work in pattern: *Purl 2 rnds, knit 2 rnds*;
rep * to *.

Rep the pattern sequence a total of 11
(12, 13, 14) times.

Now shape cap by decreasing on *every
3rd rnd* as follows:
Decrease Rnd 1 (do not decrease for size
6–12 months): *K6, k2tog*; rep * to * around.
Note: Now begin decreasing on all sizes.
Decrease Rnd 2: *K5, k2tog*; rep * to *
around, ending with K2 (0, 0, 0).
Decrease Rnd 3: *K4, k2tog*; rep * to *
around, ending with K2 (0, 0, 0).
Decrease Rnd 4: *K2, k2tog*; rep * to *
around, ending with K0 (2, 2, 3).

Decrease Rnd 5: *K1, k2tog*; rep * to *
around, ending with K0 (2, 2, 3).
Knit 1 rnd, purl 2 rnds.
Decrease Rnd 6: *K1, k2tog*; rep * to *
around, ending with K2 (2, 2, 0).
Last Decrease Rnd: *k2tog*; rep * to *
around.

Cut yarn, draw end through rem sts;
tighten.

BRIM
With WS facing, pick up and knit 26 (28, 30,
32) sts centered at front.
Purl 1 row. Continue back and forth in
stockinette. On the 10th (12th, 14th, 14th)
row, decrease as follows:
Decrease Row 1: K1, sl 1, k1, psso, knit until
3 sts rem, k2tog, k1.
Purl 1 row.
Decrease Row 2: K1, sl 1, k1, psso, knit until
3 sts rem, k2tog, k1.

Next Row: BO purlwise.
With crochet hook, work sc all around brim
and then sew brim to cap.
Sew a button in each corner.

EARFLAPS (MAKE BOTH ALIKE)
Knit earflaps on 3 smallest sizes. The
earflaps are placed inside the brim.

Flaps: With RS facing, pick and knit 17
(19, 20) sts. Purl 1 row, knit 1 row , purl 1
row.

Now decrease on every RS row as
follows:
K1, sl 1, k1, psso, knit until 3 sts rem,
k2tog, k1.
When 3 sts rem, knit an I-cord about 8
(8¾, 8¾) in [20 (22, 22) cm] long (I-cord, see
page 127).

FINISHING
Weave in all ends neatly on WS.
Lay damp towel on cap and leave until
completely dry.

Golden Summer Rompers, color 1013.

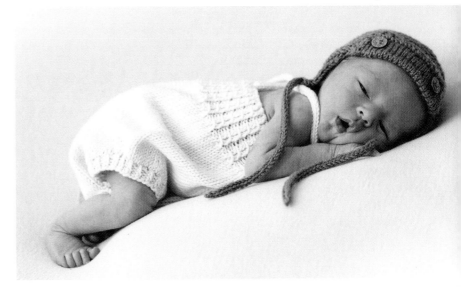

Felted Slippers in a Jiffy
(High Version)

The name says it all. Quick to make and good and warm on the feet. You can choose to make them with or without an added sole and in either a high or short version.

SIZES: 1–3 months (3–6, 9–12 months, 1-2 years)

MATERIALS
YARN: Sandnes Garn Tove [CYCA #2 – sport, 100% wool, 175 yd (160 m) / 50 g]
YARN COLORS AND AMOUNTS:
Color A: 3511: 50 (50, 50, 50) g
Color B: 2652: 50 (50, 50, 50) g
NEEDLES: US size 8 (5 mm): 16 in (40 cm) circular or set of 5 dpn
CROCHET HOOK: US size 7 (4.5 mm)
NOTIONS: fine cord or leather cord

GAUGE: 18 sts = 4 in (10 cm).
Adjust needle size to obtain correct gauge if necessary.

The slippers are worked back and forth and then seamed under the sole and up the back when finishing. A fine cord or leather cord is threaded (or sewn) through the slippers to tie them.

With either short circular or dpn, CO 27 (31, 35, 37) sts.
Purl 1 row.
Increase Row 1: K1, M1, k12 (14, 16, 17), M1, k1, M1, k12 (14, 16, 17), M1, k1.
Purl 1 row.
Increase Row 2: K1, M1, k13 (15, 17, 18), M1, k3, M1, k13 (15, 17, 18), M1, k1.
Purl 1 row.
Increase Row 3: K1, M1, k14 (16, 18, 19), M1, k5, M1, k14 (16, 18, 19), M1, k1.
Purl 1 row.
Increase Row 4: K1, M1, k15 (17, 19, 20), M1, k7, M1, k15 (17, 19, 20), M1, k1.
Purl 1 row, knit 1 row, purl 1 row, knit 1 row, purl 1 row.

Decrease Row 1: K17 (19, 21, 22), k2tog, k7, k2tog, k17 (19, 21, 22).
Purl 1 row.
Decrease Row 2: K16 (18, 20, 21), k2tog, k7, k2tog, k16 (18, 20, 21).
Purl 1 row.

Size 1-3 months only:
Decrease Row 3: K15, k2tog, k1, k2tog, k1, k2tog, k1, k2tog, k15.
Purl 1 row.

Sizes 3–6 (9–12 months, 1–2 years) only:
Decrease Row 3: K17 (19, 20), k2tog, k7, k2tog, k17 (19, 20).
Purl 1 row.
Decrease Row 4: K16 (18, 19), k2tog, k2tog, k3, k2tog, k2tog, k16 (18, 19).
Purl 1 row.

All sizes:
Next row: K15 (16, 18, 19), k2tog, sl 1, k2tog, psso, k2tog, k15 (16, 17, 19).
Purl 1 row.
Next row: K13 (14, 16, 17), k2tog, sl 1, k2tog, psso, k2tog, k13 (14, 16, 17).
Next row: P14 (15, 17, 18), BO 1 st, p14 (15, 17, 18).

Now work the 14 (15, 17, 18) sts on each side separately.

LEFT SIDE
Next row: K12 (13, 15, 16), k2tog.
Purl 1 row.
Next row: K8 (9, 11, 12), k2tog, yo, k3.
Purl 1 row, knit 1 row, purl 1 row.
Next row: K8 (9, 11, 12), k2tog, yo, k3.
Purl 1 row.
Next row: K11 (12, 14, 15), k2tog.
Purl 1 row.
Next row: K10 (11, 13, 14), k2tog.
Last row: BO purlwise.

RIGHT SIDE
Next row: Sl 1, k1, psso, k12 (13, 15, 16).
Purl 1 row.
Next row: K3, yo , sl 1, k1, psso, k8 (9, 11, 12).
Purl 1 row, knit 1 row, purl 1 row.
Next row: K3, yo, sl 1, k1, psso, k8 (9, 11, 12).
Purl 1 row.

Next row: Sl 1, k1, psso, k11 (12, 14, 15). Purl 1 row.

Purl 1 row.
Next row: Sl 1, k1, psso, k10 (11, 13, 14).
Last row: BO purlwise.

FINISHING
Seam back and sole of slipper. Weave in all ends neatly on WS. Make 2nd slipper the same way.

OPTIONAL CROCHETED SOLE
Use hook US size 7 (4.5 mm)
Rnd 1: Ch 11 (12, 14, 15). Work 4 dc in the 9th (10th, 12th, 13th) ch and then 1 dc in each of the next 8 (9, 11, 12) ch back to beginning, and 5 dc in the 1st ch.

Work 1 dc in each ch on other side of ch. Join to 1st dc with 1 sl st.

Rnd 2: Ch 2, 1 dc in next st, 2 dc in 3rd st, 1 dc in each of next 6 (7, 9, 10) sts, 1 tr in each of next 2 sts, 2 tr in each of next 5 sts, 1 tr in each of next sts, 1 dc in each of next 6 (7, 9, 10) sts. Join to 1st dc with 1 sl st.

Rnd 3: Ch 1, 1 sc in 1st st, 2 sc in each of next 4 sts, 1 sc in each of next 11 (12, 15, 17) sts, 2 sc in each of next 5 sts, 1 sc in each st to beginning of rnd. Join to 1st sc with 1 sl st. Sew sole to slipper with same color yarn as sole.

ABBREVIATIONS
ch = chain stitch
dc = double crochet
sc = single crochet
sl st = slip stitch
tr = treble crochet

FELTING
Felt the slippers in the washing machine. Set the machine to the regular colored cycle at 122°F (50°C). Toss in a small hand towel or something similar with the slippers. Use a wool-safe soap. If possible, set to a high spin cycle.

After felting, the slipper soles should measure approx. 4 (4¼, 4¾, 5¼) in [10 (11, 12, 13) cm]. If they are too big, run them through another washer cycle.

Felted Slippers in a Jiffy
(Short Version)

SIZES: 1–3 months (3–6, 9–12 months, 1–2 years)

MATERIALS
YARN: Sandnes Garn Tove [CYCA #2 – sport, 100% wool, 175 yd (160 m) / 50 g]
YARN COLORS AND AMOUNTS:
Color A: 1035: 50 (50, 50, 50) g
Color B: 2652: 50 (50, 50, 50) g
NEEDLES: US size 8 (5 mm): 16 in (40 cm) circular or set of 5 dpn
CROCHET HOOK: US size 7 (4.5 mm)
NOTIONS: leather cord or something similar, about 10½ in (26 cm) long; 2 buttons

GAUGE: 18 sts = 4 in (10 cm).
Adjust needle size to obtain correct gauge if necessary.

The slippers are worked back and forth and then seamed under the sole and up the back when finishing.

With either short circular or dpn, CO 27 (31, 35, 37) sts.
   Purl 1 row.
   Increase Row 1: K1, M1, k12 (14, 16, 17), M1, k1, M1, k12 (14, 16, 17), M1, k1.
   Purl 1 row.
   Increase Row 2: K1, M1, k13 (15, 17, 18), M1, k3, M1, k13 (15, 17, 18), M1, k1.
   Purl 1 row.
Increase Row 3: K1, M1, k14 (16, 18, 19), M1, k5, M1, k14 (16, 18, 19), M1, k1.
   Purl 1 row.
Increase Row 4: K1, M1, k15 (17, 19, 20), M1, k1, M1, k5, M1, k1, k15 (17, 19, 20), M1, k1.
   Purl 1 row, knit 1 row, purl 1 row, knit 1 row, purl 1 row.

Decrease Row 1: K17 (19, 21, 22), k2tog, k7, k2tog, k17 (19, 21, 22).
   Purl 1 row.
Decrease Row 2: K16 (18, 20, 21), k2tog, k7, k2tog, k16 (18, 20, 21).
Purl 1 row.

Size 1–3 months only:
Decrease Row 3: K15, k2tog, k1, k2tog, k1, k2tog, k1, k2tog, k15.
Purl 1 row.

Sizes 3–6 (9–12 months, 1–2 years) only:
Decrease Row 3: K17 (19, 20), k2tog, k7, k2tog, k17 (19, 20).
Purl 1 row.
Decrease Row 4: K16 (18, 19), k2tog, k2tog, k3, k2tog, k2tog, k16 (18, 19).
Purl 1 row.

All sizes:
Next row: K15 (16, 18, 19), k2tog, sl 1, k2tog, psso, k2tog, k15 (16, 17, 19).
Purl 1 row. sl 1,
Next row: K13 (14, 16, 17), k2tog, sl 1, k2tog, psso, k2tog, k13 (14, 16, 17).
Last row: BO purlwise.

FINISHING
Seam back and sole of slipper.
Weave in all ends neatly on WS.
Make 2nd slipper the same way.

OPTIONAL CROCHETED SOLE
Use hook US size 7 (4.5 mm)
Rnd 1: Ch 11 (12, 14, 15). Work 4 dc in the 9th (10th, 12th, 13th) ch and then 1 dc in each of the next 8 (9, 11, 12) ch back to beginning, and 5 dc in the 1st ch.
   Work 1 dc in each ch on other side of ch. Join to 1st dc with 1 sl st.

Rnd 2: Ch 2, 1 dc in next st, 2 dc in 3rd st, 1 dc in each of next 6 (7, 9, 10) sts, 1 tr in each of next 2 sts, 2 tr in each of next 5 sts, 1 tr in each of next 2 sts, 1 dc in each of next 6 (7, 9, 10) sts. Join to 1st dc with 1 sl st.

Rnd 3: Ch 1, 1 sc in 1st st, 2 sc in each of next 4 sts, 1 sc in each of next 11 (12, 15, 17) sts, 2 sc in each of next 5 sts, 1 sc in each st to beginning of rnd. Join to 1st sc with 1 sl st. Sew sole to slipper with same color yarn as sole.

ABBREVIATIONS
ch = chain stitch
dc = double crochet
sc = single crochet
sl st = slip stitch
tr = treble crochet

FELTING
Felt the slippers in the washing machine. Set the machine to the regular colored cycle at 122°F (50°C). Toss in a small hand towel or something similar with the slippers. Use a wool-safe soap. If possible, set to a high spin cycle.
   After felting, the slipper soles should measure approx. 4 (4¼, 4¾, 5¼) in [10 (11, 12, 13) cm]. If they are too big, run them through another washer cycle.

TIES
Use a leather cord or something similar, 5¼ in (13 cm) long. Fold cord and wrap yarn around the end. Using yarn, sew cord securely to 1 side of the slipper (see photo above). On the other side, sew on a button.

Albert Cap

A new KlompeLompe favorite for the whole family. The structure of the cap makes it unbelievably fun to knit.

Level 2

SIZES: Newborn (1–2, 3–6, 6–9 months, 1–2 , 3–6, 8–12 years, adult S/M, Adult L/XL)

MATERIALS
Sandnes Garn KlompeLompe Merinoull (Merino wool) [CYCA #3 – DK, light worsted, 100% Merino wool, 114 yd (104 m) / 50 g]
YARN COLORS AND AMOUNTS:
Color 1042: 50 (50, 50, 50, 100, 100, 100, 100, 100) g
NEEDLES: US sizes 2.5 and 4 (3 and 3.5 mm): 16 in (40 cm) circulars and set of 5 dpn (larger size only)

GAUGE: 22 sts on larger-size needles = 4 in (10 cm).
Adjust needle size to obtain correct gauge if necessary.

Winter Pine Cone Pullover: color A 6571,
color B 6521, color C 7251

With smaller-size circular, CO 60 (66, 72, 76, 80, 84, 88, 94, 98) sts. Join, being careful not to twist cast-on row; pm for beginning of rnd. Work 8 (8, 8, 8, 10, 10, 12 12, 12) rnds k1, p1 ribbing.

Change to larger-size circular. Knit 1 rnd, increasing 4 (6, 8, 4, 8, 4, 8, 10, 14) sts evenly spaced around = 64 (72, 80, 80, 88, 88, 96, 104, 112) sts.

Now work in pattern.

Note: On sizes 1–2 months and 1–2 years, work Rnds 1–4 once before beginning the 1st rnd.

On sizes 3–6 months, 3–6 years, and adult S/M, work Rnds 11–20 once before beginning the 1st rnd.

Pattern (multiple of 8 sts; repeat to specified or desired length)

Rnd 1: *P3, k2, p3*; rep * to * around.
Rnd 2: *P3, sl 2, p3*; rep * to * around.
Rnd 3: *P3, k2, p3*; rep * to * around.
Rnd 4: *P3, sl 2, p3*; rep * to * around.
Rnd 5: *P2, 1/1RPC, 1/1LPC, p2*; rep * to * around.
Rnd 6: *P2, sl 1, p2, sl 1, p2*; rep * to * around.
Rnd 7: *P1, 1/1RPC, p2, 1/1LPC, p1*; rep * to * around.
Rnd 8: *P1, sl 1, p4, sl 1, p1*; rep * to * around.
Rnd 9: *1/1RPC, p4, 1/1LPC *; rep * to * around.
Rnd 10: *Sl 1, p6, sl 1*; rep * to * around.
Rnd 11: *K1, p6, k1*; rep * to * around.
Rnd 12: *Sl 1, p6, sl 1*; rep * to * around.
Rnd 13: *K1, p6, k1*; rep * to * around.
Rnd 14: *Sl 1, p6, sl 1*; rep * to * around.
Rnd 15: *1/1LPC, p4, 1/1RPC *; rep * to * around.
Rnd 16: *P1, sl 1, p4, sl 1, p1*; rep * to * around.
Rnd 17: *P1, 1/1LPC, p2, 1/1RPC, p1*; rep * to * around.
Rnd 18: *P2, sl 1, p2, sl 1, p2*; rep * to * around.
Rnd 19: *P2, 1/1LPC, 1/1RPC, p2*; rep * to * around.
Rnd 20: *P3, sl 2, p3*; rep * to * around.

STITCHES AND TECHNIQUES

1/1RPC

Option 1: Skip 1st st but leave it on needle. Knit 2nd st in front of 1st st. Purl 1st st.
Option 2: Slip st st to cable needle and hold in back of work. Knit 2nd st (in front of st on cable needle). Purl st on cable needle.

1/1LPC

Option 1: Skip 1st st but leave it on needle. Purl 2nd st behind 1st st. Knit 1st st.
Option 2: Slip st st to cable needle and hold in front of work. Purl 2nd st (behind st on cable needle). Knit st on cable needle.

CROWN SHAPING

On the 2nd (2nd, 2nd, 3rd, 3rd, 3rd, 4th, 5th, 5thx) time of working complete pattern repeat, work the 6th rnd as follows:
Decrease Rnd 1 (Rnd 6): *P2tog, sl 1, p2, sl 1, p2tog*; rep * to * around.
Rnd 7: *1/1RPC, p2, 1/1LPC*; rep * to * around.
Rnd 8: *Sl 1, p4, sl 1*; rep * to * around.
Rnd 9: * K1, p4, k1*; rep * to * around.
Decrease Rnd 2 (Rnd 10): *Sl 1, p1, p2tog, p1, sl 1*; rep * to * around.
Rnd 11: *K1, p3, k1*; rep * to * around.
Decrease Rnd 3 (Rnd 12): *Sl 1, p2tog, p1, sl 1*; rep * to * around.
Rnd 13: *K1, p2, k1*; rep * to * around.
Decrease Rnd 4 (Rnd 14): *Sl 1, p2tog, sl 1*; rep * to * around.
Rnd 15: *K1, p1, k1*; rep * to * around.
Decrease Rnd 5 (Rnd 16): *K1, k2tog*; rep * to * around.
Last rnd: *K2tog*; rep * to * around.

FINISHING

Cut yarn, draw end through rem sts; tighten.
Weave in all ends neatly on WS.
Lay damp towel on cap and leave until completely dry.

If desired, sew on a fake fur pom-pom or make a pom-pom and sew it on.

Albert Mittens for Children

Lovely mittens with an easy but impressive pattern. These can also be knitted in adult sizes (see next pattern) so everyone in the family can have a pair.

SIZES: 1–2 (3–5, 6–8, 10–14) years

MATERIALS
Sandnes Garn KlompeLompe Merinoull (Merino wool) [CYCA #3 – DK, light worsted, 100% Merino wool, 114 yd (104 m) / 50 g]
YARN COLORS AND AMOUNTS:
Color 1013: 50 (50, 50, 100) g
NEEDLES: US size 4 (3.5 mm): set of 5 dpn or 32 in (80 cm) circular for magic loop (magic loop: see video at klompelompe.no)

GAUGE: 22 sts = 4 in (10 cm).
Adjust needle size to obtain correct gauge if necessary.

CO 32 (32, 40, 48) sts. Divide sts onto dpn and join.

Purl 1 rnd, knit 1 rnd, purl 1 rnd, knit 1 rnd.

Begin working pattern:

Begin on Rnd 1 (11, 3, 1) the 1st time and then rep pattern Rnds 1–20.

Pattern (repeat to specified or desired length)
Rnd 1: *P3, k2, p3*; rep * to * around.
Rnd 2: *P3, sl 2, p3*; rep * to * around.
Rnd 3: *P3, k2, p3*; rep * to * around.
Rnd 4: *P3, sl 2, p3*; rep * to * around.
Rnd 5: *P2, 1/1RPC, 1/1LPC, p2*; rep * to * around.
Rnd 6: *P2, sl 1, p2, sl 1, p2*; rep * to * around.
Rnd 7: *P1, 1/1RPC, p2, 1/1LPC, p1*; rep * to * around.
Rnd 8: *P1, sl 1, p4, sl 1, p1*; rep * to * around.
Rnd 9: *1/1RPC, p4, 1/1LPC *; rep * to * around.
Rnd 10: *Sl 1, p6, sl 1*; rep * to * around.
Rnd 11: *K1, p6, k1*; rep * to * around.
Rnd 12: *Sl 1, p6, sl 1*; rep * to * around.
Rnd 13: *K1, p6, k1*; rep * to * around.
Rnd 14: *Sl 1, p6, sl 1*; rep * to * around.
Rnd 15: *1/1LPC, p4, 1/1RPC *; rep * to * around.
Rnd 16: *P1, sl 1, p4, sl 1, p1*; rep * to * around.
Rnd 17: *P1, 1/1LPC, p2, 1/1RPC, p1*; rep * to * around.
Rnd 18: *P2, sl 1, p2, sl 1, p2*; rep * to * around.
Rnd 19: *P2, 1/1LPC, 1/1RPC, p2*; rep * to * around.
Rnd 20: *P3, sl 2, p3*; rep * to * around.

STITCHES AND TECHNIQUES
1/1RPC
Option 1: Skip 1st st but leave it on needle. Knit 2nd st in front of 1st st. Purl 1st st.
Option 2: Slip st st to cable needle and hold in back of work. Knit 2nd st (in front of st on cable needle). Purl st on cable needle.

1/1LPC
Option 1: Skip 1st st but leave it on needle. Purl 2nd st behind 1st st. Knit 1st st.
Option 2: Slip st st to cable needle and hold in front of work. Purl 2nd st (behind st on cable needle). Knit st on cable needle.

Continue in pattern until mitten measures 3¼ (3¼, 4, 4) in [8 (8, 10, 10) cm]. Now use a smooth contrast color yarn to mark thumbhole:

RIGHT MITTEN
Work 1 st in pattern, k6 with waste yarn, slide the 6 sts back to left needle and knit with working yarn. Work rem of rnd in pattern.

Winter Pine Cone Pullover: color A 7251, color
B 1013, color C 6521
Pilot Cap's Little Brother: color 2652

LEFT MITTEN

Work palm, 9 (9, 13, 17) sts in pattern, k6 with waste yarn, slide the 6 sts back to left needle and knit with working yarn. Work rem of rnd in pattern.

On the 3rd (3½th, 4th, 4th) time working pattern, work the 6th rnd as follows:
Decrease Rnd 1 (Rnd 6): *P2tog, sl 1, p2, sl 1, p2tog*; rep * to * around.
Rnd 7: *1/1RPC, p2, 1/1LPC*; rep * to * around.
Decrease Rnd 2 (Rnd 8): *Sl 1, p2tog, p2tog, sl 1*; rep * to * around.
Rnd 9: * K1, p2, k1*; rep * to * around.

Decrease Rnd 3 (Rnd 10): *Sl 1, p2tog, sl 1*; rep * to * around.
Rnd 11: *K1, p1, k1*; rep * to * around.
Last rnd: *K2tog*; rep * to * around.
Cut yarn, draw end through rem sts; tighten.

THUMB

Insert dpn into 6 sts below waste yarn and then another dpn into 6 sts above waste yarn. Pick up 1 st at each side = 14 sts. Carefully remove waste yarn. Divide sts onto dpn or magic loop circular. Purl around for 1½ (2, 2½, 2¾) in [4 (5, 6, 7) cm].
Last rnd: *P2tog*; rep * to * around.
Cut yarn, draw end through rem sts; tighten.

FINISHING

Weave in all ends neatly on WS.
If necessary sew up any holes at sides of thumb.
Lay damp towel on mittens and leave until completely dry.

Albert Mittens for Adults

SIZES: Women's (Men's)

MATERIALS
Sandnes Garn KlompeLompe Merinoull (Merino wool) [CYCA #3 – DK, light worsted, 100% Merino wool, 114 yd (104 m) / 50 g]
YARN COLORS AND AMOUNTS:
Color 4344: 100 (150) g
NEEDLES: US size 4 (3.5 mm): set of 5 dpn or 32 in (80 cm) circular for magic loop (magic loop: see video at klompelompe.no)

GAUGE: 22 sts = 4 in (10 cm).
Adjust needle size to obtain correct gauge if necessary.

CO 48 (56) sts. Divide sts onto dpn and join.
   Purl 1 rnd, knit 1 rnd, purl 1 rnd, knit 1 rnd.
   Begin working pattern:
   Begin on Rnd 11 (1) the 1st time and then rep pattern Rnds 1–20.

Pattern (repeat to specified or desired length)
Rnd 1: *P3, k2, p3*; rep * to * around.
Rnd 2: *P3, sl 2, p3*; rep * to * around.
Rnd 3: *P3, k2, p3*; rep * to * around.
Rnd 4: *P3, sl 2, p3*; rep * to * around.
Rnd 5: *P2, 1/1RPC, 1/1LPC, p2*; rep * to * around.
Rnd 6: *P2, sl 1, p2, sl 1, p2*; rep * to * around.
Rnd 7: *P1, 1/1RPC, p2, 1/1LPC, p1*; rep * to * around.
Rnd 8: *P1, sl 1, p4, sl 1, p1*; rep * to * around.
Rnd 9: *1/1RPC, p4, 1/1LPC *; rep * to * around.
Rnd 10: *Sl 1, p6, sl 1*; rep * to * around.
Rnd 11: *K1, p6, k1*; rep * to * around.
Rnd 12: *Sl 1, p6, sl 1*; rep * to * around.

Rnd 13: *K1, p6, k1*; rep * to * around.
Rnd 14: *Sl 1, p6, sl 1*; rep * to * around.
Rnd 15: *1/1LPC, p4, 1/1RPC *; rep * to * around.
Rnd 16: *P1, sl 1, p4, sl 1, p1*; rep * to * around.
Rnd 17: *P1, 1/1LPC, p2, 1/1RPC, p1*; rep * to * around.
Rnd 18: *P2, sl 1, p2, sl 1, p2*; rep * to * around.
Rnd 19: *P2, 1/1LPC, 1/1RPC, p2*; rep * to * around.
Rnd 20: *P3, sl 2, p3*; rep * to * around.

STITCHES AND TECHNIQUES

1/1RPC

Option 1: Skip 1st st but leave it on needle. Knit 2nd st in front of 1st st. Purl 1st st.
Option 2: Slip st st to cable needle and hold in back of work. Knit 2nd st (in front of st on cable needle). Purl st on cable needle.

1/1LPC

Option 1: Skip 1st st but leave it on needle. Purl 2nd st behind 1st st. Knit 1st st.
Option 2: Slip st st to cable needle and hold in front of work. Purl 2nd st (behind st on cable needle). Knit st on cable needle.

Continue in pattern until mitten measures 4¾ (5¼) in [12 (13.5) cm]. Now use a smooth contrast color yarn to mark thumbhole:

RIGHT MITTEN

Work 1 st in pattern, k7 with waste yarn, slide the 7 sts back to left needle and knit with working yarn. Work rem of rnd in pattern.

LEFT MITTEN

Work palm, 16 (20) sts in pattern, k7 with waste yarn, slide the 7 sts back to left needle and knit with working yarn. Work rem of rnd in pattern.

On the 5½th (6th) time working pattern, work the 6th rnd as follows:
Decrease Rnd 1 (Rnd 6): *P2tog, sl 1, p2, sl 1, p2tog*; rep * to * around.
Rnd 7: *1/1RPC, p2, 1/1LPC*; rep * to * around.

Decrease Rnd 2 (Rnd 8): *Sl 1, p2tog, p2tog, sl 1*; rep * to * around.
Rnd 9: * K1, p2, k1*; rep * to * around.
Decrease Rnd 3 (Rnd 10): *Sl 1, p2tog, sl 1*; rep * to * around.
Rnd 11: *K1, p1, k1*; rep * to * around.
Last rnd: *K2tog*; rep * to * around.
Cut yarn, draw end through rem sts; tighten.

THUMB

Insert dpn into 7 sts below waste yarn and then another dpn into 7 sts above waste yarn. Pick up 1 st at each side = 16 sts. Carefully remove waste yarn. Divide sts onto dpn or magic loop circular. Purl around for 2¾ (3¼) in [7 (8) cm].
Last rnd: *P2tog*; rep * to * around.
Cut yarn, draw end through rem sts; tighten.

FINISHING

Weave in all ends neatly on WS.
If necessary sew up any holes at sides of thumb.
Lay damp towel on mittens and leave until completely dry.

Kernels Cap

A nice baggy cap with a comfy grain kernel structure and good fit.

SIZES: 1–2 (3–6, 8–12 years, adult)

MATERIALS
Sandnes Garn KlompeLompe Merinoull (Merino wool) [CYCA #3 – DK, light worsted, 100% Merino wool, 114 yd (104 m) / 50 g]
YARN COLORS AND AMOUNTS:
Color 2024: 100 (100, 150, 150) g
NEEDLES: US sizes 4 and 6 (3.5 and 4 mm): 16 in (40 cm) circulars and set of 5 dpn in larger size

GAUGE: 22 sts on US size 6 (4 mm) needles = 4 in (10 cm).
Adjust needle size to obtain correct gauge if necessary.

With short circular, CO 80 (80, 88, 88) sts. Join, being careful not to twist cast-on row; pm for beginning of rnd.
Work 12 rnds in k1, p1 ribbing.
Change to larger-size dpn, Knit 1 rnd.
Purl 1 rnd, increasing 10 (10, 12, 12) sts evenly spaced around (increase with M1p) = 90 (90, 100, 100) sts.
Now work in pattern.

PATTERN
Rnd 1: *K1, p4, yo, k1, yo, p4*; rep * to * around.
Rnd 2: *K1, p4, yo, k3, yo, p4*; rep * to * around.
Rnd 3: *K1, p4, yo, k5, yo, p4*; rep * to * around.
Rnd 4: *K1, p4, yo, k7, yo, p4*; rep * to * around.
Rnd 5: *K1, p4, yo, k9, yo, p4*; rep * to * around.
Rnd 6: *K1, p4, sl 1, k1, psso, k7, k2tog, p4*; rep * to * around.
Rnd 7: *K1, p4, sl 1, k1, psso, k5, k2tog, p4*; rep * to * around.
Rnd 8: *K1, p4, sl 1, k1, psso, k3, k2tog, p4*; rep * to * around.
Rnd 9: *K1, p4, sl 1, k1, psso, k1, k2tog, p4*; rep * to * around.
Rnd 10: *K1, p4, sl 1, k2tog, psso, p4*; rep * to * around.
Rnd 11: *Yo, k1, yo, p4, k1, p4*; rep * to * around.
Rnd 12: *Yo, k3, yo, p4, k1, p4*; rep * to * around.
Rnd 13: *Yo, k5, yo, p4, k1, p4*; rep * to * around.
Rnd 14: *Yo, k7, yo, p4, k1, p4*; rep * to * around.
Rnd 15: *Yo, k9, yo, p4, k1, p4*; rep * to * around.
Rnd 16: * Sl 1, k1, psso, k7, k2tog, p4, k1, p4*; rep * to * around.
Rnd 17: * Sl 1, k1, psso, k5, k2tog, p4, k1, p4*; rep * to * around.
Rnd 18: * Sl 1, k1, psso, k3, k2tog, p4, k1, p4*; rep * to * around.
Rnd 19: * Sl 1, k1, psso, k1, k2tog, p4, k1, p4*; rep * to * around.
Rnd 20: * Sl 1, k2tog, psso, p4, k1, p4*; rep * to * around.

Work pattern 1.5 (2, 2, 2.5) times (so that last rnd in pattern is Rnd 10 (20, 20, 10).
Change to dpn when sts no longer fit around circular.

Now work next 2 (2, 6, 2) rnds as: *K1, p4*; rep * to * around.
Decrease Rnd 1: *K1, p2tog, p2*; rep * to * around.
Work next 2 rnds as: *K1, p3*; rep * to * around.
Decrease Rnd 2: *K1, p2tog, p1*; rep * to * around.
Work next 2 rnds as: *K1, p2*; rep * to * around.
Decrease Rnd 3: *K1, p2tog, k1, p2*; rep * to * around.
Work next 2 rnds as: *K1, p1, k1, p2*; rep * to * around.
Decrease Rnd 4: *K1, p1, k1, p2tog*; rep * to * around.
Work next rnd as: *K1, p1*; rep * to * around.
Decrease Rnd 5: *K2tog tbl*; rep * to * around.

FINISHING
Cut yarn and draw end through rem sts; tighten.
Weave in all ends neatly on WS.
Lay damp towel on cap and leave until completely dry.

164

Little Miracle Coverlet

Every time a new treasure comes into the world, it is like a little miracle!
You really can't have too many coverlets to tuck around your little miracle.
Knit a coverlet for big sister's dolls first to practice the pattern and then knit
one for the the baby carriage or the baby. We offer three sizes to choose from.

Level 2

SIZES: coverlet for doll (baby carriage, baby)

FINISHED MEASUREMENTS
Doll coverlet: Approx. 15¾ x 19¾ in [40 x 50 cm]
Baby carriage coverlet: Approx. 26¾ x 31½ in [68 x 80 cm]
Baby coverlet: Approx. 31½ x 35½ in [80 x 90 cm]

MATERIALS
Sandnes Garn KlompeLompe Merinoull (Merino wool) [CYCA #3 – DK, light worsted, 100% Merino wool, 114 yd (104 m) / 50 g]
YARN COLORS AND AMOUNTS:
Color 1015 or 6521: 150 (400, 500) g
NEEDLES: US size 6 (4 mm): 32 in (80 cm) circular

GAUGE: 22 sts = 4 in (10 cm).
Adjust needle size to obtain correct gauge if necessary.

CO 67 (125, 137) sts. Work back and forth in seed st (Row 1: (K1, p1) across. On all following rows, work knit over purl and purl over knit).

Now work in pattern, continuing seed st over the outermost 5 (10, 10) sts at each side.

Note: Pattern (does not include the 5 (10, 10) edge sts at each side.

Row 1 (RS): P1, *(k1, p1, k1, p1, k1) in next st, p3*; rep * to * across.
Row 2: *K3, p5*; rep * to * across until 1 st rem, k1.
Row 3: P1, *k5, p3*; rep * to * across.
Row 4: *K3, p5*; rep * to * across until 1 st rem, k1.
Row 5: P1, *sl 1, k1, psso, k1, k2tog, p3*; rep * to * across.
Row 6: *K3, p3*; rep * to * across until 1 st rem, k1.
Row 7: P1, *sl 1, k2tog, psso, p1, (k1, p1, k1, p1, k1) in next st, p1*; rep * to * across.

Row 8: K1, *p5, k3*; rep * to * across.
Row 9: *P3, k5*; rep * to * across until 1 st rem, p1.
Row 10: K1, *p5, k3*; rep * to * across.
Row 11: P3, *sl 1, k1, psso, k1, k2tog *; rep * to * across until 1 st rem, k1.
Row 12: K1, *p3, k3*; rep * to * across.
Row 13: P1, *(k1, p1, k1, p1, k1) in next st, p1, sl 1, k2tog, psso , p1*; rep * to * across.
Rep Rows 2–13 until coverlet measures approx. 17¾ (24¾, 29½) in [45 (63, 75) cm] and the next row is Row 13 in pattern. Now work as follows:
P1, *p2, sl 1, k2tog, psso, p1*; rep * to * across.

End with 8 (20, 20) rows seed st; BO in seed st on last row.

FINISHING
Weave in all ends neatly on WS. Dampen coverlet, pat out to finished measurements and lay it in a towel until dry. Optional: steam- press under a damp pressing cloth.

Christmas

Fredrik Sweater-Jacket
for Children

A classic block-pattern sweater. It's easy to knit and has only minimal finishing. It goes well with a dressy outfit.

SIZES: 1 (2, 4, 6, 8, 10, 12) years

FINISHED MEASUREMENTS
Chest: Approx. 20 (21½, 23¾, 25¾, 27¼, 30, 32¼) in [51 (54.5, 58, 65.5, 69, 76, 82) cm]
Length: Approx. 13½ (15¾, 17¾, 19¼, 20½, 21¾, 22¾) in [34 (40, 45, 49, 52, 55, 58) cm]

MATERIALS
Sandnes Garn KlompeLompe Merinoull (Merino wool) [CYCA #3 – DK, light worsted, 100% Merino wool, 114 yd (104 m) / 50 g]
YARN COLORS AND AMOUNTS:
Color 6061: 250 (300, 300, 350, 400, 450, 550) g
NEEDLES: US size 6 (4 mm): 24 and 32 in (60 and 80 cm) circulars (magic loop: see video at klompelompe.no; set of 5 dpn
NOTIONS: 4 (4, 5, 5, 5, 6, 6) buttons

GAUGE: 22 sts = 4 in (10 cm).
Adjust needle size to obtain correct gauge if necessary.

The sweater is worked back and forth, beginning at lower edge.

CO 190 (198, 216, 230) sts.
Work back and forth in k1, p1 ribbing for 3¼ in (8 cm).
Purl 1 row, dividing for front and back as follows: p42 (44, 48, 51), pm, p106 (110, 120, 128), pm, p42 (44, 48, 51).
Now work front pieces in block pattern and back in stockinette.

BLOCK PATTERN
Rows 1–4: Rep *k4, p4* until 2 (4, 0, 3) sts rem, k2 (4, 0, 3), work back in stockinette, p2 (4, 0, 3) , rep *k4, p4* to end of row.
Rows 5–8: Knit front sts on all rows (= garter ridges), work back in stockinette.
Rows 9–12: Rep *p4, k4* until 2 (4, 0, 3) sts rem, p2 (4, 0, 3), work back in stockinette, k2 (4, 0, 3) , rep *p4, k4* to end of row.
Rows 13–16: Knit front sts on all rows (= garter ridges), work back in stockinette.

Continue in pattern as est until body measures approx. 17 (17¾, 19, 19¾) in [43 (45, 48, 50) cm] and you've just worked Row 7 or 15 in pattern. On the next row (WS): shape armholes:
Work 38 (40, 44, 47) sts in pattern, BO 8 sts, p98 (102, 112, 120), BO 8 sts, 38 (40, 44, 47) sts in pattern.

Set body aside while you knit sleeves.

SLEEVES
With dpn, CO 52 (56, 60, 62) sts. Divide sts onto dpn and join; pm for beginning of rnd.
Work around in k1, p1 ribbing for 3¼ in (8 cm).
The sleeves are worked in block pattern throughout.
Note: On Rnds 5–8 and 13–16: Knit 1 rnd, purl 1 rnd, knit 1 rnd, purl 1 rnd for garter ridges.
When sleeve measures 4¾ in (12 cm), increase 1 st on each side of marker as follows: K1, M1, work until 1 st before marker, M1, k1. Work new sts into pattern.
Increase the same way approx. every ⅝ in (1.5 cm) until you have 94 (96, 102, 108) sts.
Continue without further increasing until sleeve is 19¾ in (50 cm) long.
On next rnd, BO 8 sts centered on under-arm. Set sleeve aside while you knit 2nd sleeve the same way.

JOIN BODY AND SLEEVES
Arrange body and sleeves on circular = 346 (358, 388, 414) sts total. Pm at each intersection of body ad sleeve.

Work 6 rows back and forth, continuing as est with block pattern on front and stockinette on back.

Before proceeding, read the next 2 sections carefully.

NECKBAND/COLLAR

Pick up and knit sts along right front and up to center back—about 3 sts for every 4 sts/rows. Begin picking up sts at lower edge so that the 1st row begins at back neck. Work back and forth in garter st (= knit every row) for a total of 26 (26, 26, 28) rows. On the next row (at back), k85 (85, 90, 95); turn and knit back. Turn and knit until 5 sts before previous turn; turn and knit back. Continue turning and knitting until 5 sts before previous turn a total of 12 (12, 13, 14) times = 24 (24, 26, 28) rows. Turn and knit 1 row; BO.

Work left side of collar the same way but make buttonholes on every 12th (12th, 12th) row as follows: Begin at lower edge, k4, BO 2 sts (CO 2 new sts over each gap on next row). Make a total of 6 (7, 7, 7) buttonholes spaced about 2⅜ in (6 cm) apart.

FINISHING

Seam collar at back neck and seam underarms. Sew on buttons.
Weave in all ends neatly on WS.
Lay sweater under a damp towel and leave until completely dry.

On the next row (RS), decrease as follows: *Work until 2 sts before marker, k2tog tbl, k2tog*; rep * to * across, working to end of row after last decrease = 8 sts decreased. Decrease the same way on every RS row a total of 28 (30, 32, 35) times.

At the same time, on every 4th row (always a RS row), decrease 1 st at beginning and end of row as follows: K1, k2tog, work until 3 sts rem, k2tog, k1. Rep this decrease a total of 12 (10, 12, 12) times.

When all decreases have been worked, 98 (98, 108, 110) sts rem.

Knit 1 row and BO.

Fredrik Sweater-Jacket for Men

A sweater-jacket for men, knitted with lovely Merino wool yarn. This sweater has a striking silhouette and the easy block pattern is an elegant detail.

SIZES: S (M, L, XL)

FINISHED MEASUREMENTS
Chest: Approx. 33¼ (34¾, 37¾, 41) in [84.5 (88, 96, 104) cm]
Length: Approx. 26¾ (27½, 29½, 31) in [68 (70, 75, 79) cm]
MATERIALS
Sandnes Garn KlompeLompe Merinoull (Merino wool) [CYCA #3 – DK, light worsted, 100% Merino wool, 114 yd (104 m) / 50 g]
YARN COLORS AND AMOUNTS:
Color 6571: 700 (750, 800, 900) g
NEEDLES: US size 6 (4 mm): 32 in (80 cm) circulars (magic loop: see video at klompelompe.no; set of 5 dpn
NOTIONS: 6 (7, 7, 7) buttons

GAUGE: 22 sts = 4 in (10 cm).
Adjust needle size to obtain correct gauge if necessary.

The sweater is worked back and forth, beginning at lower edge.

CO 190 (198, 216, 230) sts.
Work back and forth in k1, p1 ribbing for 3¼ in (8 cm).
Purl 1 row, dividing for front and back as follows: p42 (44, 48, 51), pm, p106 (110, 120, 128), pm, p42 (44, 48, 51).
Now work front pieces in block pattern and back in stockinette.

BLOCK PATTERN
Rows 1–4: Rep *k4, p4* until 2 (4, 0, 3) sts rem, k2 (4, 0, 3), work back in stockinette, p2 (4, 0, 3), rep *k4, p4* to end of row.
Rows 5–8: Knit front sts on all rows (= garter ridges), work back in stockinette.
Rows 9–12: Rep *p4, k4* until 2 (4, 0, 3) sts rem, p2 (4, 0, 3), work back in stockinette, k2 (4, 0, 3) , rep *p4, k4* to end of row.
Rows 13–16: Knit front sts on all rows (= garter ridges), work back in stockinette.

Continue in pattern as est until body measures approx. 17 (17¾, 19, 19¾) in [43 (45, 48, 50) cm] and you've just worked Row 7 or 15 in pattern. On the next row (WS): shape armholes:
Work 38 (40, 44, 47) sts in pattern, BO 8 sts, p98 (102, 112, 120), BO 8 sts, 38 (40, 44, 47) sts in pattern.

Set body aside while you knit sleeves.

SLEEVES
With dpn, CO 52 (56, 60, 62) sts. Divide sts onto dpn and join; pm for beginning of rnd.
Work around in k1, p1 ribbing for 3¼ in (8 cm).
The sleeves are worked in block pattern throughout.
Note: On Rnds 5–8 and 13–16: Knit 1 rnd, purl 1 rnd, knit 1 rnd, purl 1 rnd for garter ridges.
When sleeve measures 4¾ in (12 cm), increase 1 st on each side of marker as

follows: K1, M1, work until 1 st before marker, M1, k1. Work new sts into pattern.
Increase the same way approx. every ⅝ in (1.5 cm) until you have 94 (96, 102, 108) sts.
Continue without further increasing until sleeve is 19¾ in (50 cm) long.
On next rnd, BO 8 sts centered on underarm. Set sleeve aside while you knit 2nd sleeve the same way.

JOIN BODY AND SLEEVES
Arrange body and sleeves on circular = 346 (358, 388, 414) sts total. Pm at each intersection of body ad sleeve.

Work 6 rows back and forth, continuing as est with block pattern on front and stockinette on back.

Before proceeding, read the next 2 sections carefully.

On the next row (RS), decrease as follows: *Work until 2 sts before marker, k2tog tbl, k2tog*; rep * to * across, working to end of row after last decrease = 8 sts decreased. Decrease the same way on every RS row a total of 28 (30, 32, 35) times.

At the same time, on every 4th row (always a RS row), decrease 1 st at beginning and end of row as follows: K1, k2tog, work until 3 sts rem, k2tog, k1. Rep this decrease a total of 12 (10, 12, 12) times.

When all decreases have been worked, 98 (98, 108, 110) sts rem.

Knit 1 row and BO.

NECKBAND/COLLAR

Pick up and knit sts along right front and up to center back—about 3 sts for every 4 sts/rows. Begin picking up sts at lower edge so that the 1st row begins at back neck. Work back and forth in garter st (= knit every row) for a total of 26 (26, 26, 28) rows. On the next row (at back), k85 (85, 90, 95); turn and knit back. Turn and knit until 5 sts before previous turn; turn and knit back. Continue turning and knitting until 5 sts before previous turn a total of 12 (12, 13, 14) times = 24 (24, 26, 28) rows. Turn and knit 1 row; BO.

Work left side of collar the same way but make buttonholes on every 12th (12th, 12th) row as follows: Begin at lower edge, k4, BO 2 sts (CO 2 new sts over each gap on next row). Make a total of 6 (7, 7, 7) buttonholes spaced about 2⅜ in (6 cm) apart.

FINISHING

Seam collar at back neck and seam underarms. Sew on buttons.
Weave in all ends neatly on WS.
Lay sweater under a damp towel and leave until completely dry.

Christmas Dress

A single-color dress with a textured pattern
inspired by traditional knitting.

Level 2

SIZES: 0–1 (3, 6, 9, 12, 18, 24, 36) months

FINISHED MEASUREMENTS
Chest: Approx. 15¾ (17½, 17½, 19¼, 19¼,
20½, 21, 23¼) in [40 (44.5, 44.5, 49, 49, 52,
53.5, 59) cm]
Total Length: Approx. 12¼ (13, 13¾, 14½,
15, 15¾, 17¾, 18½) in [31 (33, 35, 37, 38, 40,
45, 47) cm]

MATERIALS
YARN: Sandnes Garn KlompeLompe Tynn
Merinoull (fine Merino wool) [CYCA #1 –
fingering, 100% Merino wool, 191 yd (175 m)
/ 50 g]
YARN COLORS AND AMOUNTS:
Color 6571: 100 (150, 150, 150, 150, 200,
200, 200) g
NEEDLES: US sizes 1.5 and 2.5 (2.5 and 3
mm): 16 and 24 in (40 and 60 cm) circulars
and sets of 5 dpn or 32 in (80 cm) magic
loop circular (magic loop: see video at
klompelompe.no)
CROCHET HOOK: US D-3 (3 mm)
NOTIONS: 3 (3, 3, 3, 4, 4, 4, 4) buttons

GAUGE: 27 sts on larger-size needles = 4 in
(10 cm).
Adjust needle size to obtain correct gauge
if necessary.

The dress is worked from the top down,
beginning back and forth on a circular
needle.

With smaller-size circular, CO 64 (68, 68,
72, 76, 80, 84, 84) sts, Knit 5 rows back and
forth in garter st; the 1st row = WS. Change
to larger-size circular.

Knit 1 row, increasing (with kf&b) 16 (12, 12,
16, 20, 16, 12, 12) sts evenly spaced across
= 80 (80, 80, 88, 96, 96, 96, 96) sts.

Purl 1 row.
   Now begin pattern following chart A.
   Knit 2 rows (= 1 garter ridge). Knit 1 row,
increasing 24 (32, 32, 32, 32, 32, 32, 32) sts
evenly spaced across = 104 (112, 112, 120,
128, 128, 128, 128) sts. Purl 1 row.

Work chart B.
   Knit 2 rows (= 1 garter ridge). Knit 1 row,
increasing 40 sts evenly spaced across =
144 (152, 152, 160, 168, 168, 168, 168) sts.
Purl 1 row.

Sizes 12 (18, 24, 36) months: Work chart
A. Knit 2 rows (= 1 garter ridge). Knit 1 row,
increasing 24 (24, 24, 32) sts evenly spaced
across = 192 (192, 192, 200) sts. Purl 1 row.

All sizes:
   Work chart C.
   Knit 2 rows (= 1 garter ridge). Knit 1 row,

increasing 20 (28, 36, 32, 12, 16, 28, 28) sts
evenly spaced across = 164 (180, 188, 192,
204, 208, 220, 228) sts. Purl 1 row.

From this point on, work around on a circular
needle. Knit 1 (2, 4, 6, 1, 2, 4, 6) rnds.
   Place sleeve sts on holders: k23 (26, 27,
28, 30, 31, 33, 34), place next 36 (38, 40, 40,
42, 42, 44, 46) sts on holder, CO 8 sts for
underarm, k46 (52, 54, 56, 60, 62, 66, 68),
place next 36 (38, 40, 40, 42, 42, 44, 46) sts
on holder, CO 8 sts for underarm, k23 (26,
27, 28, 30, 31, 33, 34) = 108 (120, 124, 128,
136, 140, 148, 152) sts rem for body.

Knit 3 (4, 6, 6, 8, 8, 10, 10) rnds and, on 1st
rnd, adjust st count to 108 (120, 120, 132,
132, 140, 144, 160 sts. Purl 1 rnd, knit 2 rnds.
Eyelet Rnd:
   Sizes 0–1 (3, 6, 9, 12, 24) months: K1,
k2tog, yo, *k4, k2tog, yo: rep * to * around
until 3 sts rem, k3.
Size 18 months: K1, k2tog, yo, *k5, k2tog,
yo: rep * to * around until 4 sts rem, k4.
Size 36 months: K2, k2tog, yo, *k6, k2tog,
yo: rep * to * around until 4 sts rem, k4.

Knit 2 rnds, purl 1 rnd.
   Knit 1 rnd, adjusting st count to 112 (120,
120, 136, 136, 144, 144, 160 sts.
   Knit 1 rnd, placing markers as follows:
K1 (seed st), pm, *k12 (13, 13, 15, 15, 16, 16,
18), pm, k2 (seed st). pm*; rep * to * until 13
(14, 14, 16, 16, 17, 17, 19) sts rem, k12 (13,
13, 15, 15, 16, 17, 18), pm, k1 (seed st).

Chart A

← Begin here

Chart B

Chart C

← Begin here

← Begin here

←←
Christmas Top
color 6061

Now work seed st (begin with k1, p1 and, on subsequent rnds, work knit over purl and purl over knit) in seed st sections and stockinette over rem sts.

After 2 rnds, increase as follows: 1 seed st, increase 1 with M1 (twisted knit or purl to fit into seed st pattern), *k12 (13, 13, 15, 15, 16, 16, 18), M1, 2 seed sts, M1*; rep * to * until 13 (14, 14, 16, 16, 17, 18, 19) sts rem, k12 (13, 13, 15, 15, 16, 16, 18), M1, k1 (seed st).

Each seed st section should now have 4 sts.

Now increase 1 st at beginning and 1 st at end of each seed st section.

Increase after 4 rnds and then after 8 rnds. Increase again after 8 rnds and then after 12 rnds.

Increase again every 18th rnd until each seed st section has 12 (14, 14, 16, 16, 18, 18, 20) sts.

Continue without further increasing until dress measures 11¾ (12¾, 13½, 14¼, 14½, 15½, 17¼, 18¼) in [30 (32, 34, 36, 37, 39, 44, 46) cm]. Change to smaller-size circular and work 3 ridges: purl 1 rnd, knit 1 rnd, purl 1 rnd, knit 1 rnd. **Last rnd:** BO purlwise.

Knitting Tip: If the bind-off seems too tight, use the larger-size circular for last rnd.

SLEEVES

Change to smaller-size needle. Knit 5 rows back and forth (1st row = WS). Sew ends of the ridges to dress.

BACK OPENING

With crochet hook, work sc all around opening. Turn and work sl st back, making 3 (3, 3, 3, 4, 4, 4, 4) buttonholes evenly spaced on left side. Buttonhole: Ch 5, attach ch with sl st. Make top buttonhole at neck edge.

FINISHING

Weave in all ends neatly on WS. Lay damp towel over dress and leave until completely dry. Twist a yarn cord and thread through eyelet rnd.

Winter-Fine Overalls

Our first cap was the Kjekka cap. Inspired by the textured pattern on the cap, we designed the overalls. Perfect for crawling around in.

Change to larger-size dpn. Knit 1 rnd, increasing 17 sts evenly spaced around = 57 (57, 61, 61, 65, 65, 65) sts.

Pm as follows: K20 (20, 22, 22, 24, 24, 24), pm, work 17 sts in pattern, pm, k20 (20, 22, 22, 24, 24, 24).

Continue in stockinette except for the 17 pattern sts.

When leg is 1¼ in (3 cm) above ribbing, increase as follows:

K1, M1, work as est until 1 st rem, M1, k1.

Increase the same way every ¾ in (2 cm) a total of 4 (5, 6, 7, 8, 9, 10) times = 65 (67, 73, 75, 81, 83, 85) sts.

Continue as est without further increasing until leg measures 4¼ (5½, 6¾, 7½, 8¼, 9, 9¾) in [11 (14, 17, 19, 21, 23, 25) cm] from change to larger-size needles.

Set leg aside while you make 2nd leg the same way.

Arrange the legs on a circular so that the pattern sections face the sides:

CO 3 sts, work sts of 1 leg, CO 6 sts, work 2nd leg, CO 3 sts.

The beginning of the rnd is at center back. Pm on each side of the 4 center sts of front and back = 142 (146, 158, 162, 174, 178, 182) sts.

Work 3 rnds. On next rnd, decrease as follows:

K2, k2tog tbl, work until 2 sts before marker at center front, k2tog, k4, k2tog tbl, work until 2 sts before center back marker, k2tog, k2. Decrease the same way every 3rd rnd a total of 5 times = 122 (126, 138, 142, 154, 158, 162) sts rem.

When piece measures 4¾ (5¼, 5½, 6, 6, 6¼, 6¼) in [12 (13 14, 15, 15, 16, 16) cm] above cast-on sts between legs, raise the back with short rows (after each turn, make a yarnover and, when you come to a yarnover later, knit/purl it with next st).
K20; turn, p40; turn, k36; turn, p32; turn, k28; turn, p24; turn, k12 (you are now at beginning of the rnd).

SIZES: 0–1 (1–3, 6, 9 months, 1, 2, 3 years)

FINISHED MEASUREMENTS
Chest: Approx. 17¾ (18½, 20, 21, 22½, 23¼, 23¾) in [45 (47, 51, 53, 57, 59, 60) cm]
Total Length: Approx. 19 (20, 22¼, 24¾, 26½, 28¼, 31) in [48 (51, 56.5, 63, 67, 72, 79) cm]

MATERIALS
YARN: Sandnes Garn KlompeLompe Tynn Merinoull (fine Merino wool) [CYCA #1 – fingering, 100% Merino wool, 191 yd (175 m) / 50 g]

YARN COLORS AND AMOUNTS:
Color 6571: 100 (150, 150, 150, 200, 200, 200) g
NEEDLES: US sizes 1.5 and 2.5 (2.5 and 3 mm): 16 in (40 cm) circulars and sets of 5 dpn or 32 in (80 cm) magic loop circular (magic loop: see video at klompelompe.no)
NOTIONS: 6 (6, 6, 6, 6, 6, 6) buttons

GAUGE: 27 sts on larger-size needles = 4 in (10 cm).
Adjust needle size to obtain correct gauge if necessary.

The garment begins at the lower edge and is worked in the round on dpn or magic loop.

With smaller-size dpn, CO 40 (40, 44, 44, 48, 48, 48) sts. Divide sts onto dpn and join; pm for beginning of rnd.

Work 18 (18, 20, 20, 20, 22, 22, 22) rnds k1, p1 ribbing.

Pattern (for pattern section)
Row 1: *P1, k1*; rep * to * until 1 st rem in pattern section, p1.
Row 2: Work as for Rnd 1.
Row 3: Knit.
Row 4: Purl.

Continue around with pattern at the sides until piece measures 8¾ (9¾, 10¾, 11, 11¾, 12¾ 14¼) in [22 (25, 27, 28, 30, 32, 36) cm] above cast-on sts between legs. BO 7 sts on each side (centered on each pattern section) for sleeves = 54 (56, 62, 64, 70, 72, 74) sts rem for each half.

Work the rem 5 pattern sts as follows:

Rows 1–2: P1, k1, p1, k1, p1 (or, on WS, k1, p1, k1, p1, k1).

Row 3: Knit (purl on WS).

Row 4: Purl (knit on WS).

BACK

Work back and forth. There should be 5 pattern sts at each side. The 1st row = WS.

Next Row (RS, decrease): 5 sts in pattern, k2tog, knit until 7 sts rem sl 1, k1, psso, 5 sts in pattern.

Decrease the same way on every RS row 5 (6, 6, 7, 7, 7, 8) times = 10 (12, 12, 14, 14, 14, 16) sts decreased = 44 (44, 50, 50, 56, 58, 58) sts rem.

Continue until 2¾ (3¼, 3½, 4, 4¾, 5¼, 5½) in [7 (8, 9, 10, 12, 13, 14) cm] above underarm.

Next row (RS): 5 sts in pattern, k10 (10, 12, 12, 14, 15, 15), knit and place 14 (14, 16, 16, 18, 18, 18) sts on a holder, k10 (10, 12, 12, 14, 15, 15), 5 sts in pattern = 15 (15, 17, 17, 19, 20, 20) sts rem for each shoulder

Now decrease at neck edge:

LEFT SHOULDER

Continue in pattern over the 5 pattern sts and stockinette on the 10 (10, 12, 12, 14, 15, 15) sts rem sts.

The 1st row = WS.

Next row (RS): K2tog, work as est to end of row.

Decrease the same way on every RS row a total of 3 times. After working last decrease row, with smaller-size needle, work 5 rows in k1, p1 ribbing; BO on last row.

RIGHT SHOULDER

Continue in pattern over the 5 pattern sts and stockinette on the 10 (10, 12, 12, 14, 15, 15) sts rem sts.

The 1st row = WS.

Next row (RS): Work as est until 2 sts rem, sl 1, k1, psso.

Decrease the same way on every RS row a total of 3 times. After working last decrease row, with smaller-size needle, work 5 rows in k1, p1 ribbing; BO on last row.

NECKBAND RIBBING

With US size 1.5 (2.5 mm) needle, pick up and knit about 10 sts on each side of the 14 (14, 16, 16, 18, 18, 18) sts on holder.

Work 5 rows k1, p1 ribbing; BO on in ribbing on last row.

FRONT

Work back and forth. There should be 5 pattern sts at each side. The 1st row = WS.

Next row (RS, decrease): 5 sts in pattern, k2tog, knit until 7 sts rem sl 1, k1, psso, 5 sts in pattern.

Decrease the same way on every RS row 5 (6, 6, 7, 7, 7, 8) times = 10 (12, 12, 14, 14, 14, 16) sts decreased = 44 (44, 50, 50, 56, 58, 58) sts rem.

Continue 2 (2⅜, 2½, 3, 3½, 4, 4) in [5 (6, 6.5, 7.5, 9, 10, 10) cm] above underarm.

Next row (RS): 5 sts in pattern, k10 (10, 12, 12, 14, 15, 15), knit and place 14 (14, 16, 16, 18, 18, 18) sts on a holder, k10 (10, 12, 12, 14, 15, 15), 5 sts in pattern = 15 (15, 17, 17, 19, 20, 20) sts rem for each shoulder.

Now decrease at neck edge:

RIGHT SHOULDER

Continue in pattern over the 5 pattern sts and stockinette on the 10 (10, 12, 12, 14, 15, 15) sts rem sts.

The first row = WS.

Next Row (RS): K2tog, work as est to end of row.

Decrease the same way on every RS row a total of 3 times. After working last decrease row, work as est for ¾ (¾, 1, 1, 1¼, 1¼, 1½) in (2, 2.5, 2.5, 3, 3, 4) cm] without decreasing. With US size 1.5 (2.5 mm) needle, work 5 rows in k1, p1 ribbing; BO on last row, but, on 2nd row, make 2 buttonholes with k2tog, yo.

LEFT SHOULDER

Continue in pattern over the 5 pattern sts and stockinette on the 10 (10, 12, 12, 14, 15, 15) sts rem sts.

The first row = WS.

Next Row (RS): Work as est until 2 sts rem, sl 1, k1, psso.

Decrease the same way on every RS row a total of 3 times. After working last decrease row work as est for ¾ (¾, 1, 1, 1¼, 1¼, 1½) in (2, 2.5, 2.5, 3, 3, 4) cm] without decreasing. With US size 1.5 (2.5 mm) needle, work 5 rows in k1, p1 ribbing; BO on last row, but, on 2nd row, make 2 buttonholes with k2tog, yo.

NECKBAND RIBBING

With smaller size needle, pick up and knit 16 (16, 19, 19, 20, 20, 21) sts on each side of the 14 (14, 16, 16, 18, 18, 18) sts on holder. Work 5 rows k1, p1 ribbing; BO on in ribbing on last row, but make a buttonhole at each end up at the shoulder.

FINISHING

Weave in all ends neatly on WS.
Sew 3 buttons on each shoulder. Seam crotch.

Lay a damp towel over overalls and leave until completely dry or gently steam-press under a damp pressing cloth.

Christmas Rompers

A romper version of the Christmas dress on bigger-size needles.
It gives us a nostalgic feeling.

SIZES: 0–1 (3, 6, 9, 12, 18, 24, 36) months

FINISHED MEASUREMENTS
Chest: Approx. 16½ (19¼, 21, 21, 21¾, 25¼, 26½, 27¼) in [42 (49, 53, 53, 55.5, 64, 67, 69) cm]
Total Length: Approx. 11½ (13¾, 15½, 16½, 18¼, 19¾, 21¼, 22) in [29 (35, 39, 42, 46, 50, 54, 56) cm]

MATERIALS
YARN: Sandnes Garn Duo [CYCA #3 – DK, light worsted, 55% Merino wool, 45% cotton, 126 yd (115 m) / 50 g]
YARN COLORS AND AMOUNTS:
Color 6032: 100 (150, 150, 150, 150, 150, 200, 200) g
NEEDLES: US sizes 2.5 and 4 (3 and 3.5 mm): 16 and 24 in (40 and 60 cm) circulars (smaller size only uses shorter needle)
CROCHET HOOK: US size E-4 (3.5 mm)
NOTIONS:
8 (8, 8, 8, 8, 8, 8, 8) buttons

GAUGE: 22 sts on larger-size needles = 4 in (10 cm).
Adjust needle size to obtain correct gauge if necessary.

Beginning back and forth on a circular needle, the rompers are worked from the top down.

With smaller-size circular, CO 60 (66, 66, 66, 70, 70, 74, 74) sts.
Knit 5 rows (= garter ridges). The 1st row = WS.

Change to larger-size circular. Knit 1 rnd, increasing (increase with kf&b) 20 (14, 14, 14, 18, 18, 22, 22) sts evenly spaced across = 80 (80, 80, 80, 88, 88, 96, 96) sts.

All sizes except 0–1 month
Purl 1 row. Work chart A.
Knit 2 rows (= garter ridge).
Knit 1 row increasing—(24, 32, 32, 32, 32, 32, 32) sts evenly spaced across = (104, 112, 112, 120, 120, 128, 128) sts.

All sizes:
Purl 1 row. Work chart B. Knit 2 rows (= garter ridge).
Knit 1 row increasing 40 (40, 40, 40, 40, 40, 40, 40) sts evenly spaced across = 120 (144, 152, 152, 160, 160, 168, 168) sts.

Sizes 18 (24, 36) months:
Purl 1 row. Work chart A. Knit 2 rows (= garter ridge).
Knit 1 row increasing – (–, –, –, –, 32, 32, 40) sts evenly spaced across = – (–, –, –, –, 192, 200, 208) sts.

Purl 1 row. Work chart C. Knit 2 rows (= garter ridge). Knit 1 row.
On the next row, join to work in the round; pm for beginning of rnd. BO for sleeves as follows:
K20 (24, 26, 26, 28, 32, 34, 35), BO purlwise 20 (24, 24, 24, 24, 32, 32, 34) sts, k40 (48, 52, 52, 56, 64, 68, 70), BO purlwise 20 (24, 24, 24, 24, 32, 32, 34) sts, k20 (24, 26, 26, 28, 32, 34, 35).

Knit 1 rnd, and, *at the same time*, CO 6 sts over each underarm = 92 (108, 116, 116, 124, 140, 148, 152) sts.
Pm centered on each underarm. Knit 1 rnd.
Now work short rows to raise the back. (After a turn, make a yarnover, and, when you come to the yarnover later, knit st/purl it together with following st.)
K10; turn, p20; turn, k25; turn, p30; turn, k35; turn, p40; turn, k20 (now you are at beginning of rnd).

Continue around in stockinette. When piece is ¾ in (2 cm) below underarm, increase at each marker: *Knit until 2 sts before marker, M1, knit until 2 sts after marker, M1*; rep * to * = 4 sts increased. Increase the same way every ¾ in (2 cm) a total of 5 times = 112 (128, 136, 136, 144, 160, 168, 172) sts.

Continue in stockinette until piece measures 6 (7, 8¼, 9, 10¼, 11, 11¾, 12¾) in [15 (18, 21, 23, 26, 28, 30, 32) cm] below underarms.

Color 2652

DIVIDE BODY FOR LEGS

K13 (16, 17, 17, 18, 20, 21, 23), place next 34 (36, 38, 38, 40, 44, 46, 45) sts on a holder, k18 (24, 26, 26, 28, 32, 34, 36), place next 34 (36, 38, 38, 40, 44, 46, 45) sts on a holder, k13 (16, 17, 17, 18, 20, 21, 23).

Cut yarn and place the 1st and last 13 (16, 17, 17, 18, 20, 21, 23) sts on same needle = 26 (32, 34, 34, 36, 40, 42, 46) sts for back. Work back separately, back and forth.

The 1st row = RS. Continue in stockinette. Knit 1 row, purl 1 row.

Decrease on the next row as follows: K2tog, knit until 2 sts rem, k2tog tbl. Decrease the same way on every RS row until 14 (18, 18, 18, 18, 18, 18, 18) sts rem. Purl 1 row on WS and then place sts on a holder.

Work front as for back, decreasing until 14 (18, 18, 18, 18, 18, 18, 18) sts rem.

Work ¾ in (2 cm) without decreasing and place sts on a holder. Now work each leg in the round.

LEFT LEG

With smaller-size circular, pick up and knit 10 sts on left side of front.

Work held sts as follows:

K2 (3, 4, 4, 5, 7, 8, 8), k2tog, k3, k2tog, k3, k2tog, k2tog, k2tog, k2tog, k2tog, k3, k2tog, k3, k2tog, k2 (3, 4, 4, 5, 7, 8, 7). Pick up and knit 10 sts on left side of back = 45 (47, 49, 49, 51, 55, 57, 56) sts.

Knit 5 rnds; BO on last rnd.

RIGHT LEG

Work as for left leg.

BUTTON BAND, BACK

With smaller-size needle, pick up and knit 3 sts on end of garter band around leg, knit held sts and pick up and knit 3 sts on opposite side. Knit 5 rows; BO on last row.

BUTTONHOLE BAND, FRONT

With smaller-size needle, pick up and knit 3 sts on end of garter band around leg, knit held sts and pick up and knit 3 sts on opposite side. Knit 5 rows; BO on last row. **Note:** On the 2nd row, make 4 buttonholes evenly spaced across. Buttonhole = k2tog, yo.

BACK OPENING

With crochet hook, sc all around back opening. Turn and sl st back, making 4 buttonholes evenly spaced on left side. Buttonhole = Ch 4 and attach ch with 1 sl st. Make top buttonhole at neckband.

FINISHING

Weave in all ends neatly on WS.
Sew on buttons.
Lay a damp towel over rompers and leave until completely dry.

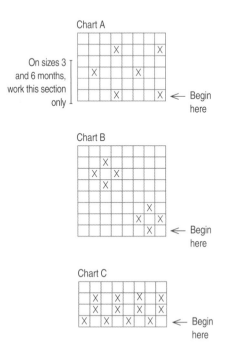

Chart A

On sizes 3 and 6 months, work this section only

← Begin here

Chart B

← Begin here

Chart C

← Begin here

☐ knit on RS, purl on WS

☒ purl on RS, knit on WS

Winter-Fine Vest

A classic vest to wear over a nice shirt.
The outfit will be perfect for winter holidays.

SIZES: 6–9 months (1, 2, 4, 6, 8) years

FINISHED MEASUREMENTS
Chest: Approx. 19¾ (21¾, 21⅞, 22½, 23¼, 25¼) in [50 (55, 55.5, 57, 59, 64) cm]
Total Length: Approx. 11¾ (13½, 14¼, 15½, 17¼, 19¼) in [30 (34, 36, 39, 44, 49) cm]

MATERIALS
YARN: Sandnes Garn KlompeLompe Tynn Merinoull (fine Merino wool) [CYCA #1 – fingering, 100% Merino wool, 191 yd (175 m) / 50 g]
YARN COLORS AND AMOUNTS:
Color 7251: 100 (100, 100, 100, 150, 150) g
NEEDLES: US sizes 1.5 and 2.5 (2.5 and 3 mm): 16 and 24 in (40 and 60 cm) circulars
NOTIONS: 6 (6, 6, 6, 6, 6) buttons

GAUGE: 27 sts on larger-size needles = 4 in (10 cm).
Adjust needle size to obtain correct gauge if necessary.

The vest begins at the lower edge and is worked in the round on a circular needle.

With smaller-size circular, CO 136 (148, 150, 154, 160, 172) sts. Join, being careful not to twist cast-on row; pm for beginning of rnd.
    Work 12 (12, 14, 14, 14, 14) rnds in k1, p1 ribbing.

Pattern for pattern section:
Rows 1–2: *P1, k1*; rep * to * to last st in section, p1.
Row 3: Knit.
Row 4: Purl.

Change to larger-size needle. Pm as follows: 17 (17, 17, 17, 21, 21) sts pattern, pm, k51 (57, 58, 60, 59, 65), pm, 17 (17, 17, 17, 21, 21) sts pattern, pm, k51 (57, 58, 60, 59, 65).
    Work pattern sections as marked and rem sts in stockinette until body measures 7½ (8¾, 9½, 10¼, 11, 12¾) in [19 (22, 24, 26, 28, 32) cm].

BO 7 sts at each side (centered over pattern) for each armhole = 61 (67, 68, 70, 73, 79) sts each for front and back.
    Pattern over rem 5 (5, 5, 7, 7) sts of pattern section as follows:
Rows 1–2: *P1, k1*; rep to * to last st, p1 (on WS, work knit over knit and purl over purl).
Row 3: Knit (purl on WS).
Row 4: Purl (knit on WS).

BACK
Work back and forth. There should now be 5 (5, 5, 5, 7, 7) pattern sts at each side. The 1st row = WS.
    Next row (RS, decrease): Work 5 (5, 5, 5, 7, 7) sts in pattern, k2tog, knit until 7 (7, 7, 7, 9, 9) sts rem, sl 1, k1, psso, work 5 (5, 5, 5, 7, 7) sts in pattern.

Decrease the same way on every RS row a total of 6 (6, 6, 7, 7, 8) times = 12 (12, 12, 14, 14, 16) sts decreased = 49 (55, 56, 56, 59, 63) sts rem.
    Continue without further decreasing until 3½ (4¾, 5¼, 5¼, 5½, 5½) in [9 (12, 13, 13, 14, 14) cm] above underarms.
Next row (RS):
Work 5 (5, 5, 5, 7, 7) sts in pattern k11 (14, 14, 14, 13, 15), place next 17 (17, 18, 18, 19, 19) sts on a holder, k11 (14, 14, 14, 13, 15), work 5 (5, 5, 5, 7, 7) sts in pattern = 16 (19, 19, 19, 20, 22) sts for each shoulder.

Now shape neck:

LEFT SHOULDER
Continue in pattern on the 5 (5, 5, 5, 7, 7) pattern sts, and in stockinette on the rem 11 (14, 14, 14, 13, 15) sts.
    The 1st row = WS.
Next row (RS, decrease): K2tog, work as est to end of row.
    Decrease the same way on every RS row a total of 3 (3, 3, 3, 3, 3) times. After last decrease row, work 5 rows in k1, p1 ribbing; BO in ribbing on last row.

RIGHT SHOULDER
Continue in pattern on the 5 (5, 5, 5, 7, 7) pattern sts, and in stockinette on the rem 11 (14, 14, 14, 13, 15) sts.
    The 1st row = WS.
Next row (RS, decrease): Work as est until 2 sts rem, sl 1, k1, psso.
Decrease the same way on every RS row a total of 3 (3, 3, 3, 3, 3) times. After last decrease row, on smaller-size needles work 5 rows in k1, p1 ribbing; BO in ribbing on last row.

BACK NECKBAND RIBBING
With smaller-size needle, pick up and knit approx. 10 sts on each side of the 17 (17, 18, 18, 19, 19) sts on holder; knit sts on holder when you come to them. Work 5 rows in k1, p1 ribbing; BO in ribbing on last row.

FRONT
Work back and forth. There should be 5 (5, 5, 5, 7, 7) pattern sts at each side. The 1st row = WS.
Next row (RS, decrease): Work 5 (5, 5, 5, 7, 7) sts in pattern, k2tog, knit until 7 (7, 7, 7, 9, 9) sts rem, sl 1, k1, psso, work 5 (5, 5, 5, 7, 7) sts in pattern.

Decrease the same way on every RS row a total of 6 (6, 6, 7, 7, 8) times = 12 (12, 12, 14, 14, 16) sts decreased = 49 (55, 56, 56, 59, 63) sts rem.

Continue without further decreasing until 2½ (3½, 4, 4, 4, 4) in [6.5 (9, 10, 10, 10, 10) cm] above underarms.

Next row (RS):
Work 5 (5, 5, 5, 7, 7) sts in pattern k11 (14, 14, 14, 13, 15), place next 17 (17, 18, 18, 19, 19) sts on a holder, k11 (14, 14, 14, 13, 15), work 5 (5, 5, 5, 7, 7) sts in pattern = 16 (19, 19, 19, 20, 22) sts for each shoulder.

Now shape neck:

RIGHT SHOULDER
Continue in pattern on the 5 (5, 5, 5, 7, 7) pattern sts, and in stockinette on the rem 11 (14, 14, 14, 13, 15) sts.

The 1st row = WS.
Next Row (RS, decrease): K2tog, work as est to end of row.

Decrease the same way on every RS row a total of 3 (3, 3, 3, 3, 3) times. After last decrease row, work 1 (1¼, 1¼, 1¼, 1½, 1½) in [2.5 (3, 3, 3, 4, 4) cm] without decreasing. On smaller-size needles, work 5 rows in k1, p1 ribbing; BO on last row. **Note:** Make 2 buttonholes on 2nd row of ribbing; buttonhole = k2tog, yo.

LEFT SHOULDER
Continue in pattern on the 5 (5, 5, 5, 7, 7) pattern sts, and in stockinette on the rem 11 (14, 14, 14, 13, 15) sts.
The 1st row = WS.
Next Row (RS, decrease): Work as est until 2 sts rem, sl 1, k1, psso.

Decrease the same way on every RS row a total of 3 (3, 3, 3, 3, 3) times. After last decrease row, work 1 (1¼, 1¼, 1¼, 1½, 1½) in [2.5 (3, 3, 3, 4, 4) cm] without decreasing. On smaller size needles, work 5 rows in k1, p1 ribbing; BO on last row. **Note:** Make 2 buttonholes on 2nd row of ribbing; buttonhole = k2tog, yo. The 3rd buttonhole is worked later in the neckband ribbing.

FRONT NECKBAND RIBBING
With smaller-size needle, pick up and knit 19 (20, 20, 20, 21, 21) sts on each side of the 17 (17, 18, 18, 19, 19) sts on holder; knit sts on holder when you come to them. On smaller-size needles, work 5 rows in k1, p1 ribbing; make a buttonhole on each end at shoulder. BO on last row.

FINISHING
Weave in all ends neatly on WS. Sew 3 buttons on each shoulder.
Lay a damp towel over rompers and leave until completely dry.

Christmas Top

A sweet Christmas top with simple details. You can easily change the look by changing the color or making it with short or long sleeves.

Level 2

Color 6061

SIZES: 6 months (9 months, 1, 2, 4, 6, 8, 10, 12, 14) years

FINISHED MEASUREMENTS

Chest: Approx. 16¼ (17½, 18¾, 21, 24½, 25½, 26¾, 30¼, 30¼, 31½) in [41.5 (44.5, 47.5, 53, 62, 65, 68, 77, 77, 80) cm]
Total Length: Approx. 7½ (8¾, 10½, 11½, 12¾, 13½, 15, 17, 17¾, 19¼) in [19 (22, 26.5, 29, 32, 34, 38, 43, 45, 49) cm]

MATERIALS

YARN: Sandnes Garn KlompeLompe Tynn Merinoull (fine Merino wool) [CYCA #1 – fingering, 100% Merino wool, 191 yd (175 m) / 50 g]

YARN COLORS AND AMOUNTS:

Color 4331: 100 (100, 150, 150, 150, 200, 250, 300, 300, 300) g

NEEDLES: US sizes 1.5 and 2.5 (2.5 and 3 mm): 16 and 24 in (40 and 60 cm) circulars and sets of 5 dpn or 32 in (80 cm) circular for magic loop (see video on magic loop at klompelompe.no)

CROCHET HOOK: US size C-2 (2.5 mm)

GAUGE: 27 sts on larger-size needles = 4 in (10 cm).
Adjust needle size to obtain correct gauge if necessary.

The top begins at the neckline and is initially worked back and forth on a circular needle.

With smaller-size circular, CO 86 (94, 94, 102, 102, 110, 110, 118, 118, 118) sts. Knit 5 rows (1st row = WS).

Change to larger-size circular. Knit 1 row, increasing 18 (18, 18, 18, 18, 18, 26, 18, 26, 26) sts evenly spaced across (work increases as kf&b) = 104 (112, 112, 120, 120, 128, 136, 136, 144, 144) sts.
    Purl 1 row and then work following chart A.

Knit 2 rows (= 1 garter ridge). Knit 1 row, increasing 32 sts evenly spaced across = 136 (144, 144, 152, 152, 160, 168, 168, 176, 176) sts.
Purl 1 row and then work following chart B.
Knit 2 rows (= 1 garter ridge). Knit 1 row, increasing 32 (40, 40, 40, 40, 40, 40, 40, 40, 40) sts evenly spaced across = 168 (184, 184, 192, 192, 200, 208, 208, 216, 216) sts.

Sizes 1, 2, 4, 6, 8, 10, 12, 14 years only:
Purl 1 row.
    Work following chart A.
    Knit 2 rows (= 1 garter ridge). *Now join to work in the round.* Pm for beginning of rnd.
    Knit 1 rnd, increasing 40 sts evenly spaced around = – (–, 224, 232, 232, 240, 248, 248, 256, 256) sts.

Size 4 years only:
Knit 1 rnd and then work following chart A.
    Knit 1 rnd, purl 1 rnd (= 1 garter ridge).
    Knit 1 rnd, increasing 32 sts evenly spaced around = 264 sts.

Sizes 6, 8, 10, 12, 14 years only:
Knit 1 rnd. Work following chart B.
    Knit 1 rnd, purl 1 rnd (= 1 garter ridge).
    Knit 1 rnd, increasing 40 sts evenly spaced around = – (–, –, –, –, 280, 288, 288, 296, 296) sts.

Sizes 10, 12, 14 years only:
Purl 1 rnd.
    Work following chart A.
    Knit 1 rnd, purl 1 rnd (= 1 garter ridge).

Knit 1 rnd, increasing 24 24, 32) sts evenly spaced around = – (–, –, –, –, –, –, 312, 320, 328) sts.

All sizes (worked in the round):
Knit 1 rnd.
    Work following chart C.
    Knit 1 rnd, increasing 16 (12, 0, 12, 4, 0, 4, 4, 0, 0) sts evenly spaced around. Purl 1 rnd.
    Knit 1 (3, 1, 3, 1, 1, 3, 1, 1, 3) rnds.
    Knit 1 rnd, placing sleeve sts on holders as follows:
    K25 (27, 29, 33, 39, 41, 43, 49, 49, 51), k42 (44, 54, 56, 56, 58, 60, 60, 62, 62) and place on holder for sleeve, k50 (54, 58, 66, 78, 82, 86, 98, 98, 102), k42 (44, 54, 56, 56, 58, 60, 60, 62, 62) and place on holder for sleeve, k25 (27, 29, 33, 39, 41, 43, 49, 49, 51).

On next rnd, CO 6 sts at each underarm = 112 (120, 128, 144, 168, 176, 184, 208, 208, 216) sts for body.
    Work around in stockinette until body measures 3½ (4¾, 6, 6¾, 7½, 8¼, 9½, 10¾, 11, 11½) in [9 (12, 15, 17, 19, 21, 24, 27, 28, 29) cm] below underarm.

Sizes 4, 6, 8, 10, 12, 14 years only:
Purl 1 rnd, knit 2 rnds.
    Work following chart A.
    Knit 1 rnd.

All sizes:
Purl 1 rnd, knit 2 rnds. Work following chart B. Knit 1 rnd.
Purl 1 rnd, knit 2 rnds, Work following chart C. Knit 1 rnd.

Work 4 garter ridges (1 ridge = knit 1 rnd, purl 1 rnd). BO on last rnd.

SHORT SLEEVES
The 1st rnd = RS.
    Slip sts of 1 sleeve to smaller-size circular; do not join. Work 5 rows k1, p1 ribbing; BO on 5th row. Stitch ends to top.

LONG SLEEVES
With larger-size dpn, CO 3 sts and then k42 (44, 54, 56, 56, 58, 60, 60, 62, 62) held sts, CO 3 sts. Join and work in the round. The 1st st is a marked st and is purled throughout.
    Work around in stockinette until sleeve is 1¼ in (3 cm) long, Now decrease 1 st on each side of marked purl st: k2tog after marked st and sl 1, k1, psso before marked st. Decrease the same way every 1¼ in (3 cm) until 44 (44, 44, 48, 48, 50, 50, 54, 56, 56) sts rem. Continue until sleeve measures 6¼ (7, 7½, 9½, 11½, 12¼, 13, 13¾, 14½, 15¾) in [16 (18, 19, 24, 29, 31, 33, 35, 37, 40) cm].
    Change to smaller-size dpn and work 5 rnds in k1, p1 ribbing. BO in ribbing on 5th rnd.

Make 2nd sleeve the same way.

Work around back neck opening in sc. Ch 4; turn and work 1 sl st in each sc. Cut yarn and fasten off.

FINISHING
Seam underarms. Weave in all ends neatly on WS.

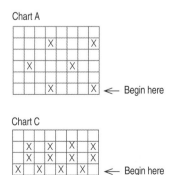

Chart A

Chart C

Chart B

☐ knit on RS, purl on WS

☒ purl on RS, knit on WS

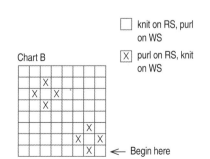

Christmas Dress color 4331

Elf Stocking Cap—Thick

A long cap with simple textured stripes. We offer two variations,
one with heavy yarn and the other with fine yarn.

SIZES: 6–12 months (1–2, 3–6, 8–12) years

MATERIALS
YARN: Sandnes Garn KlompeLompe
Merinoull (Merino wool) [CYCA #3 – DK, light
worsted, 100% Merino wool, 114 yd (104 m)
/ 50 g]
YARN COLORS AND AMOUNTS:
Color 1013: 100 (100, 100, 100) g
Pom-pom: 50 g
NEEDLES: US sizes 4 and 6 (3.5 and 4 mm):
16 in (40 cm) circulars and set of 5 dpn
in larger size or 32 in (80 cm) circular for
magic loop (see video on magic loop at
klompelompe.no)

GAUGE: 22 sts on US size 6 (4 mm) needles
= 4 in (10 cm).
Adjust needle size to obtain correct gauge
if necessary.

The cap is worked in the round on a circular
needle; the round begins at center back of
the cap.

With smaller-size circular, CO 76 (80, 84, 92)
sts. Join and pm for beginning of rnd.
Work 14 rnds in k1, p1 ribbing.
Change to larger-size circular and kni1 1 rnd,
purl 1 rnd.

Pm at each side as follows:
After 19 (20, 21, 23) sts, pm; after 38 (40, 42,
46) sts, pm; 19 (20, 21, 23) sts.

TEXTURED STRIPE PATTERN
*Knit 4 rnds.
Purl 1 rnd.*
Rep * to * for pattern.

To avoid obvious shifts on each stripe: Sl 1st
st after the purl rnd (do not knit it).

When cap measures 4¾ (5¼, 6, 6¾) in [12
(13, 15, 17) cm], begin shaping. Change to
dpn when sts no longer fit around circular.

Decrease as follows:
Decrease Rnd 1: Knit to side marker, k2tog,
knit to next side marker, k2tog.
Work 2 rnds without decreasing.

Decrease Rnd 2: Knit until 2 sts before side
marker, sl 1, k1, psso, knit until 2 sts before
next side marker, sl 1, k1, psso.
Work 2 rnds without decreasing.

NOTE If the decreases come on a purl rnd,
decrease as follows:
    Instead of k2tog, work p2tog. Instead of sl
1, k1 psso, work sl 1, p1, psso.

Repeat the 6 rnds above in stripe pattern as
est until 8 sts rem.

FINISHING
Cut yarn; draw end through rem sts; tighten.
Weave in all ends neatly on WS.
Lay a damp towel on cap and leave until
completely dry.
Make a pom-pom or use a faux fur pom-pom
to sew securely to tip of cap.

On Ludvig: color 1042

Elf Stocking Cap—Thin

SIZES: 0–2 (2–4, 4–9, 12, 18–24 months, 3–4, 5–6 years)

MATERIALS
YARN: Sandnes Garn KlompeLompe Tynn Merinoull (fine Merino wool) [CYCA #1 – fingering, 100% Merino wool, 191 yd (175 m) / 50 g]

YARN COLORS AND AMOUNTS:
Color 1013: 50 (50, 50, 50, 100, 100, 100) g
Pom-pom: 50 g

NEEDLES: US sizes 1.5 and 2.5 (2.5 and 3 mm): 16 in (40 cm) circulars and set of 5 dpn in larger size or 32 in (80 cm) circular for magic loop (see video on magic loop at klompelompe.no)

GAUGE: 27 sts on larger-size needles = 4 in (10 cm).
Adjust needle size to obtain correct gauge if necessary.

The cap is worked in the round on a circular needle; the round begins at center back of the cap.

With smaller-size circular, CO 80 (88, 92, 96, 104, 112, 120) sts. Join and pm for beginning of rnd.
Work 10 (10, 10, 12, 12, 14, 14) rnds in k1, p1 ribbing.
Change to larger-size circular and knit 1 rnd, purl 1 rnd.

Pm at each side as follows:
After 20 (22, 23, 24, 26, 28, 30) sts, pm; after 40 (44, 46, 48, 52, 56, 60) sts, pm; 20 (22, 23, 24, 26, 28, 30) sts.

<< Little Winter Pine Cone Jacket: color A 7251, color B 1013

TEXTURED STRIPE PATTERN
*Knit 4 rnds.
Purl 1 rnd.*
Rep * to * for pattern.

To avoid obvious shifts on each stripe: Sl 1st st after the purl rnd (do not knit it).

When cap measures 3½ (4, 4, 4¼, 4¾, 5¼, 5½) in [9 (10, 10, 11, 12, 13, 14) cm], begin shaping. Change to dpn when sts no longer fit around circular.

Decrease as follows:
Decrease Rnd 1: Knit to side marker, k2tog, knit to next side marker, k2tog.
Work 1 rnd without decreasing.

Decrease Rnd 2: Knit until 2 sts before side marker, sl 1, k1, psso, knit until 2 sts before next side marker, sl 1, k1, psso.

Work 1 rnd without decreasing.

NOTE: If the decreases come on a purl rnd, decrease as follows:
Instead of k2tog, work p2tog. Instead of sl 1, k1 psso, work sl 1, p1, psso.

Repeat the 4 rnds above in stripe pattern as est until 16 sts rem.
Last rnd: K2tog around.

FINISHING
Cut yarn; draw end through rem sts; tighten.
Weave in all ends neatly on WS.
Lay a damp towel on cap and leave until completely dry.
Make a pom-pom or use a faux fur pom-pom to sew securely to tip of cap.

Accessories

Crocheted Flower Leaf

MATERIALS
YARN: Sandnes Garn KlompeLompe Tynn Merinoull (fine Merino wool) [CYCA #1 – fingering, 100% Merino wool, 191 yd (175 m) / 50 g]
CROCHET HOOK: US size D-3 (3 mm)

Ch 11; turn and work 1 sl st in each chain.

Turn and work 1 dc in each of the next 2 sts, 1 tr in each of the next 5 sts, 1 dc in next st, and 1 sc in next st. End with 1 sl st in end; ch 3.

Turn and work 1 sl st in next st, 1 dc in next st, 1 tr in each of next 5 sts, 1 dc in each of next 2 sts. End with 1 sl st in end.

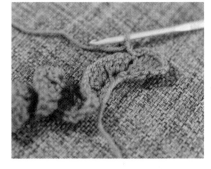

ch = chain stitch
dc = double crochet
sc = single crochet
sl st = slip stitch
tr = treble crochet

Crocheted Rose

MATERIALS
YARN: Sandnes Garn KlompeLompe Tynn Merinoull (fine Merino wool) [CYCA #1 – fingering, 100% Merino wool, 191 yd (175 m) / 50 g]
CROCHET HOOK: US size D-3 (3 mm)

Ch 27.
Ch 3 more (to substitute for 1st dc in 1st petal), and work 2 dc in the last of the 27 chain sts.

Ch 1, skip next st and work 3 dc in next st.
Rep * to * across; turn.

Ch 2, 1 dc in 1st st, 2 dc in next st, 1 dc in next st, ch 2, attach with 1 sl st around ch between petals on previous row.
Rep * to * across.

Acknowledgments

To think that we've done it again. A new knitting book has come about thanks to our fantastic, kind, and clever test knitters who helped. We would never have finished without their good help in testing out the patterns we designed for this book. Many, many thanks!

Test knitters: Ingebjørg Thorsen, Sissel Eikeland, Åse Elise Osmundsen, Ingrid Hiller, Stina Steingildra, Gunn Nordis Rafdal Ekornrud, Randi Andreassen, Johanna Gismervik, Gunnvor Thulin, Astrid A. Thorsen, Ragnhild Omvik, Siv Stonghaugen, Ida Kvalevaag, Kristine Høvring, Eva Britt Kvalevaag, Mary Therese Utvik, Gjertrud Andreassen, Inger Nes, Merete Haga Helle, Britt Alise Kvalevaag Stange, Vibeke Lindtner, Rhonda Helen Nes, Line Fossberg Taranger, Anne Linn Hovland, Synnøve Nymark,

Caroline Lillesund, Aina Kristin Størkersen, Katherine Hettervik, Tove Kalstø Milje, Liv Syre, Ingrid Gudmundsen, Ellinor Nyvoll, Kristin Ebne, Ingrid J. Dahle Bergland, Aina Pedersen, Tina Kvilhaug, Hilde Paulsen, Kristi Meyer Ånensen, Silje Kristin Berge, Linda Andrassen, Ingrid Ebne, Gro Torunn Utvik, Karen Qvale, Ida Helland, Ann-Kathrin Stalsberg, Marianne Hartwedt, Berthe Rossabø, Renate Helgen, Kristin Røyrvik, Eli Helgeland, Rakel Bergjord, Hege Hamre, Edith Helgeland Qvale, Mette Brinchmann, Liv Rasmussen, Gunn Marit Hølland.

We also want to give a big thanks this time to Sandnes Garn and Du Store Alpakkka for assisting us with yarn. Numerous skeins of yarn were used for this book project. A thousand thanks for allowing us to knit all the garments in these wonderful yarns.

Thank you again to the fantastic people at J. M. Stenersens Forlag and Kagge Forlag. Many thanks to them for being so amazingly accommodating. We also want to give a big thanks to our steadfast book designer, Anne Vines.

We are honored to recognize so many great people. Thank you to everyone who worked as models for the photos and who contributed to making this book so beautiful.

Models: Bergljot, Ingrid E, Lillian, Henry, Tora, Helene, Olivia, Hugo, Rebecca, Selma, Elina M., Britt Alise, Øystein, Tobias, Berit Margrethe, Elias, Fredrik, Camilla, Brita, Anna Elise, Elida, Liva, Sebastian, Øystein V., Ludvig, David, Linda, Theodor, Lina, Ingrid H., Marylen, Tilda, Synnøve, Elina R., Jacob, Atlas, Peter, and Erik.

Hanne Andreassen Hjelmås is a photographer with her own company. She also has two children. Hanne likes to work creatively, and her ideas for new garments mean that she often knits long into the night. Even when she is standing in line, is in the car (please note, on the passenger side), or is chatting with friends, she always has her knitting along. Color and design are what mean most for her. She takes all the photos for KlompeLompe and designs our patterns.

Torunn Steinsland was trained as a technical illustrator and works as a construction and technical designer in a consulting engineering company. She has two children. Torunn has always crocheted and learned to knit when she had a child. She likes to create unique children's clothing. Her knitting tools are always at hand, and the needles are quickly taken out when she settles in her sofa corner after a busy day.

www.klompelompe.no/en/

Index